Essential
BULATS

Business Language Testing Service

David Clark

Published in collaboration with

UNIVERSITY *of* **CAMBRIDGE**
ESOL Examinations

English for Speakers of Other Languages

CAMBRIDGE
UNIVERSITY PRESS

CAMBRIDGE UNIVERSITY PRESS
Cambridge, New York, Melbourne, Madrid, Cape Town, Singapore, São Paulo

Cambridge University Press
The Edinburgh Building, Cambridge CB2 2RU, UK

www.cambridge.org
Information on this title: www.cambridge.org/9780521618304

© Cambridge University Press 2006

First published 2006
Reprinted 2006

Printed in Italy by Legoprint S.p.A.

A catalogue record for this publication is available from the British Library

ISBN-13   978-0-521-61830-4 Student's Book with Audio CD and CD ROM
ISBN-10   0-521-61830-4 Student's Book with Audio CD and CD ROM

Contents

Introduction   4

The BULATS Listening Test   5

Part 1	PRACTICE	6–7 ✓	TEST	8–11 ✓ adapted
Part 2	PRACTICE	12–13 ✗	TEST	14–15 ✗
Part 3	PRACTICE	16–17 ✗	TEST	18 ✗ needs adapting
Part 4	PRACTICE	19–20 ✓	TEST	21–23 ✓

The BULATS Reading and Language Knowledge Test   24–25

Part 1, Section 1	PRACTICE	26–27	TEST	28–30
Part 1, Section 2	PRACTICE	31–32	TEST	33
Part 1, Section 3	PRACTICE	34–35	TEST	36–37
Part 1, Section 4	PRACTICE	38–39	TEST	40
Part 2, Section 1	PRACTICE	41–43	TEST	44–45
Part 2, Section 2	PRACTICE	46–47	TEST	48
Part 2, Section 3	PRACTICE	49–50	TEST	51
Part 2, Section 4	PRACTICE	52–53	TEST	54–55
Part 2, Section 5	PRACTICE	56–57	TEST	58–59
Part 2, Section 6	PRACTICE	60–61	TEST	62

The BULATS Writing Test   63

Part 1	PRACTICE	64	TEST	65
Part 2	PRACTICE	66	TEST	67

The BULATS Speaking Test   68–69

Part 1	PRACTICE	70	TEST	71
Part 2	PRACTICE	72	TEST	73
Part 3	PRACTICE	74	TEST	75

The BULATS Computer Test   76–77

Answer key and recording scripts   78–93

Sample Answer Sheets   94–95

Introduction

Who is this book for?

Essential BULATS is for anyone preparing to take the BULATS test. It can be used at home, or in class with a teacher.

What is in this book?

Essential BULATS covers all parts of the BULATS test.

The book covers the Standard Test (Listening, and Reading and Language Knowledge), the Writing Test and the Speaking Test. There is also an introduction to the Computer Test.

The CD ROM provides an introduction to the Computer Test. It contains the 8 question types assessed on the BULATS Computer Test. These are Listening tasks (Listen and Select; Listen and Select (graphic); and Extended Listening) and Reading and Language Knowledge tasks (Read and Select; Extended Reading; Multiple-choice gap fill; Open gap fill; and Gapped sentences). The questions on the CD ROM are exactly the same as the questions in the book, but the CD ROM allows you to try these questions on screen, in the same format as they appear in the BULATS Computer Test. However, if you prefer, you can practise these questions in the book instead.

The Audio CD contains the listening material for *Essential BULATS*.

How is this book organised?

Essential BULATS is organised by test paper (the Listening Test, the Reading and Language Knowledge Test, the Writing Test and the Speaking Test).

Each section opens with a general introduction to each part of the test. This is followed by practice material to help you prepare for each part of the test, such as skills practice and test practice. After each section there is a sample practice test on the part of the test you have just practised. The sample practice test sections are provided by Cambridge ESOL and so offer the most authentic test preparation available for BULATS.

If you prefer to take the Computer Test question types on screen, instead of in the book, these questions are provided on the CD ROM.

The answer key and recording scripts appear at the back of the book.

You can use the book in any order you wish. For example, if you would like to practise for the Reading and Language Knowledge questions, you can go directly to this section.

Further information

If you would like any further information on BULATS, please visit the website at www.BULATS.org.

The BULATS Listening Test

The BULATS Listening Test takes about 55 minutes. This includes 5 minutes at the end to transfer your answers onto a separate Answer Sheet. You can see an example of an Answer Sheet on page 94. There are 50 questions in the Listening Test. The questions, in general, become more difficult as you go through the test.

The aim of the test is to see how well you can understand spoken English and how well you can respond to it. The spoken English you will hear is in a number of different situations. All the situations are related to work and the working environment.

You will hear a mixture of people speaking: both men and women with different English accents such as British and American.

You might hear:

Monologues *1 person speaking*
- telephone messages
- public announcements (e.g. at an airport)
- parts of a business presentation
- half of a conversation (you can't hear the other person)

Dialogues *2 people speaking*
- face-to-face conversations
- telephone conversations
- interviews (e.g. a job interview)

Here is what is in each part of the test:

You will hear	Your task
1 10 short conversations or monologues 🎧 *listen twice*	• 10 multiple-choice questions (5 using pictures or graphs; 5 using written text) • 3 options for each question (A, B or C)
2 3 telephone messages or conversations 🎧 *listen once*	• 3 texts (such as an order form or a telephone message) to complete • each form has 4 spaces and you must write 1 or 2 (or sometimes 3) words in each space
3 10 short monologues 🎧 *listen once*	• match the person speaking (1–5) with the subject they are talking about (A–I)
4 3 long monologues or dialogues 🎧 *listen twice*	• 18 multiple-choice questions • 6 questions for each monologue or dialogue • 3 options for each question (A, B or C)

Listening
Understanding short extracts

You might hear:

- dates (e.g. 27th July)
- times (e.g. 10 o'clock)
- places (e.g. in reception)
- descriptions of charts and graphs (e.g. someone describing their company's sales figures)
- opinions (e.g. *I think ...*)
- people's jobs (e.g. salesperson)
- people's plans (e.g. *We're going to ...*)

Points to remember
- This part of the test concentrates on getting factual information from different listening texts.
- You will hear each recording twice, so you have a chance to check your answers the second time you listen and even to change your answer if you think it is wrong.
- The questions are multiple choice (A, B or C) so only 1 answer can be correct.
- Never leave a question unanswered. If you don't know, guess! (You have a 1 in 3 chance of being correct.)
- You will have 10 seconds to look at each question before you listen. Use this time carefully to read the question and the 3 options. Think about the information you need to find. Underline the key word(s) in the question.

Listening skills practice (picture questions)

In this section, you are going to practise listening skills

Example

1 Which is the <u>platform number</u> for the train to London?

> *These are the key words in the question.*

This is what you will hear:

> Question 1: Which is the platform number for the train to London?
>
> *Announcer:* This is an announcement for all passengers waiting for the <u>12</u> o'clock train to London Waterloo. This train will be leaving from platform <u>8</u> in <u>15</u> minutes.

The correct answer is A.

> *Often you will hear all the numbers in the recording. Only 1 is correct.*

Look at questions 2 and 3. Listen and complete the spaces in the recording script with 1 or 2 words.

2 ▢2 Which product is the company going to launch?

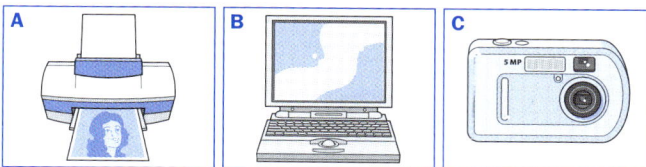

> Question 2: Which product is the company going to launch?
>
> *Manager:* And finally, I'm delighted to tell you that this year our sales have been very good. Sales of photo printers have (**a**) .... , laptops have also (**b**) .... , and we expect the HR4M digital camera (**c**) .... a great success (**d**) .... it goes on to the market (**e**) ....

3 🎧3 Which is the correct picture of the new office?

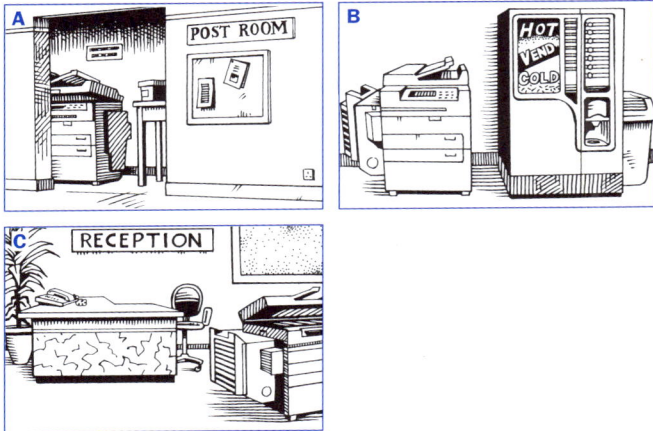

Question 3: Which is the correct picture of the new office?

Woman: What's happened to the office? I couldn't find the photocopier this morning.
Man: We made some changes while you were on holiday.
Woman: I noticed!
Man: Yes, it's (**a**) .... to the coffee machine (**b**) .... – it was too crowded sometimes during coffee breaks. We (**c**) ....
reception, but that would be too noisy.
Woman: So it's in the (**d**) .... room (**e**) ....

Test practice (picture questions)

Now try these questions. They are like the ones you will see in the test.

4 🎧4 Which graph shows the correct production figures?

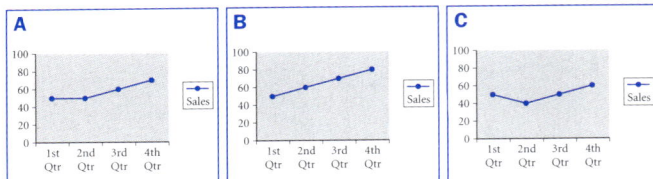

5 🎧5 What date does the sales conference start?

Test practice (text/written questions)

Example

6 Which department <u>will</u> Steve's new job be in?
  A Sales
  B Human Resources
  C Financial management

> This refers to the future. You should listen for a future plan or fact.

> Can you see all the options in the recording script below?

This is what you will hear:

Question 6: Which department will Steve's new job be in?

Woman: So, you've finished your training, Steve. Any plans?
Steve: I enjoyed the financial management training, and selling sounds interesting, but I've always liked working with people, so I'm starting in <u>Human Resources</u> on Monday.

> Only this option is talking about a future plan.

The correct answer is B.

Now try these questions.

7 🎧6 Who is the sales person talking to on the phone?
  A her boss
  B a customer
  C a supplier

> Think before you listen. What would a sales person talk to these people about?

8 🎧7 What does the announcer say about the flight to Málaga?
  A The plane has a technical problem.
  B The flight will be delayed.
  C The flight will depart soon.

> Think before you listen. What typical phrases do you hear in airport announcements?

9 🎧8 What is the manager going to do tomorrow?
  A attend a strategy meeting
  B make some phone calls
  C give a presentation

> Listen carefully to the verbs you hear. Does she say 'attend', 'make' or 'give'?

10 🎧9 Who is the man on the phone going to meet today?
  A his line manager
  B a client
  C a colleague

> Would you talk to these people in the same way?

Now do the test on pages 8–11.

Listening

Part One
Questions 1–10

- You will hear 10 short recordings.
- For questions **1–10,** circle **one** letter **A**, **B** or **C** for the correct answer.
- You will hear each recording **twice**.

1 Which pie chart is correct?

A

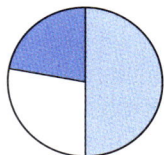

☐ Pizza bought retail
☐ Pizzas delivered to homes from takeaways
☐ Pizzas consumed in restaurants

B

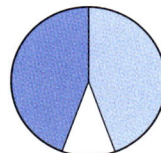

☐ Pizza bought retail
☐ Pizzas delivered to homes from takeaways
☐ Pizzas consumed in restaurants

C

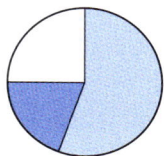

☐ Pizza bought retail
☐ Pizzas delivered to homes from takeaways
☐ Pizzas consumed in restaurants

2 Which of the products ordered are out of stock?

A

B

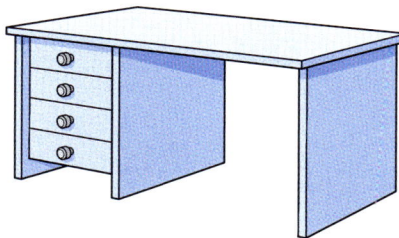

C

3 Which piece of equipment needs to be repaired?

A

B

C
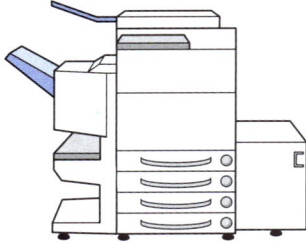

4 What is the first thing that the speaker usually does at work?

A

B

C

5 Which chart shows the correct figures?

A

% of total spending on advertising in Europe

☐ Two years ago
■ Now

35%

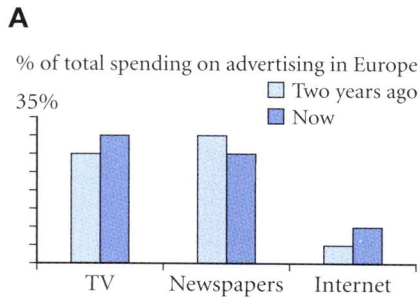

TV   Newspapers   Internet

B

% of total spending on advertising in Europe

☐ Two years ago
■ Now

35%

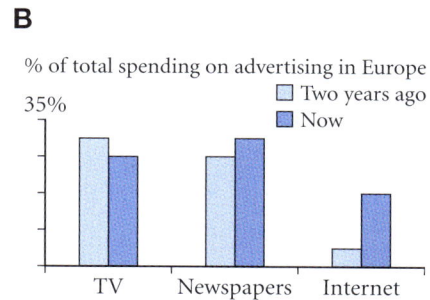

TV   Newspapers   Internet

C

% of total spending on advertising in Europe

☐ Two years ago
■ Now

35%

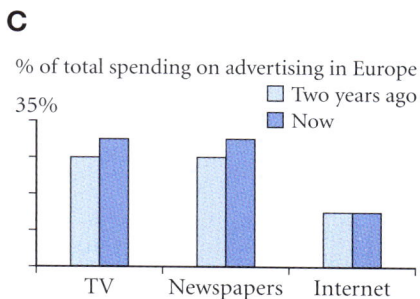

TV   Newspapers   Internet

6 What is the latest news about Peterson's?

   A It has gone out of business.

   B It has been acquired by another company.

   C It has been re-launched under a new name.

7 What is notable about the consumption of eggs by 17- to 24-year-olds?

   A They eat the highest number of eggs of all age groups.

   B The trend is different from that of most other age groups.

   C There is a difference between the numbers of males and females who eat eggs.

8 What was causing a problem for shopkeepers?

    A   the size and shape of the drinks bottles

    B   the design of the labels on the drinks bottles

    C   the strength of the containers that the drinks bottles came in

9 What is the speaker's view of the housing market?

    A   It has become less likely to show massive swings up or down.

    B   It is showing signs of being increasingly unstable.

    C   It may well suffer a huge drop in the near future.

10 What does the speaker criticise about the website?

    A   Details about the stores weren't available on the site.

    B   The company's products weren't shown in enough detail.

    C   The design of the home page wasn't consistent with other pages.

Check your answers on page 79. The recording scripts are also on page 79.

Listening Part 2

Taking down messages, notes, etc. (12 QUESTIONS)

You might have to complete:

- a note for another person (e.g. a telephone message)
- notes for you (e.g. something you need to remember in your job)
- a form (a printed document) used as part of your job, such as an order form

Points to remember
- This part of the test concentrates on factual information.
- All the answers are in the conversations or telephone messages you will hear. Write down exactly what you hear. Don't change the grammar or the vocabulary.
- There are no contractions (e.g. *can't*), possessives (e.g. *John's*) or hyphens (e.g. *high-quality*) in the answers.
- Correct spelling is important. You will lose marks for incorrect spelling. Always check your answers at the end.
- You will only hear each recording once, so be prepared for this.
- You will have 20 seconds to look at each part before you listen. Use this time carefully to read the question. Think about the information you need to find. Is it a verb? Is it a noun? Is it a number?
- The answer could be 1 or 2 (or sometimes 3) words or a number.

This is what you will see in Part 2 of the Listening Test:

Part Two
Questions 11–22
- You will hear three conversations.
- Fill in the numbered spaces, using the information you hear.
- You will hear each conversation **once** only.

The instructions for each conversation will tell you if you have to complete a form or notes.

Listening skills practice

In this section, you are going to practise listening skills

1 Look at the message and underline the answers in the recording script.

The answers appear in the recording script in the same order as the spaces on the form.

Is the answer going to be a name, a number, a noun or something else?

Message

To: Jim Carter
From: Phillip Allen, (**1**) ..Zenith... Industries
Message:
His order of (**2**) .... (50 packs), didn't arrive. Please ring him (**3**) ....
Contact details:
Call him on (**4**) ....

You won't see the recording script in the test.

Woman: Hello. Client Services. Can I help you?
Man: Yes. I'd like to speak to Jim Carter about an order we made.
Woman: I'm afraid he's not in today. Can I take a message?
Man: Yes. Could you tell him Phillip Allen from <u>Zenith</u> Industries – that's Z-E-N-I-T-H – called?
Woman: OK. And what's the message?
Man: I asked for 50 packs of printer paper last week and I expected them to be delivered yesterday, but nothing arrived.
Woman: Thanks. He'll be back late today so I'll tell him to call you tomorrow. Can I take your telephone number?
Man: Sure. He's got my office number, but he could try my mobile phone on 0343 423 7373.
Woman: OK. I'll give him your message.
Man: Thanks. Goodbye.

Check your answers on page 79.

2 🎧 **11** **Read the advice below. Then listen and complete the sentences.**

Thinking about the missing words

Before you listen: Look at each space and think about what type of word each one could be. Most of them will be nouns, but what type? Are they things? Are they places? Are they days or months?

As you listen: Write the missing words. There might be 1 or 2 (or sometimes 3) words missing in each space. Concentrate on the correct spelling because this is important in the test.

What information does an invoice have on it?

a If you give me the .... of the invoice, I can check the amount for you.

b We'd like to arrange delivery to our .... near Paris.

What do goods come in?

c We expected four .... of goods, but we have only received three of them.

d I'm afraid we won't be able to complete the project until .... at the earliest.

e One of our .... will visit you with some samples.

Who could bring product samples to your office?

f I suggest you contact the .... if you have any questions about the payment method.

g I'll be out of the office until ....

h There will be about .... at the presentation.

i What <u>are</u> the exact .... of the product?

This word is important. Why?

When you think about a product, what do you think about?

Check your answers on page 79. The recording scripts are on page 80.

Test practice

Now try these questions.

🎧 **12** **Conversation 1. Questions 1–4.**
- Look at the message below.
- You will hear a man leaving a message for your colleague about a delivery problem.

What kind of word is missing here?

What might affect company records?

Telephone Message
Message from: Pete Thompson, FX Transport
Message to: Alain
Re: your order for (1) .... supplies.

There is a problem because a (2) .... has affected their records. Please could you confirm the product (3) .... by calling 0203 4533 3455. Also, the last delivery was to the (4) .... Please also confirm if that's the case for this order, too.

Do you know any collocations with 'product'?

This must be a place. Where do deliveries sometimes go?

🎧 **13** **Conversation 2. Questions 5–8.**
- Look at the notes below.
- You will hear a man talking to a colleague about a meeting they are going to attend.

What other types of cost can projects have?

Re: Project meeting
- Remember to take information on raw material and (5) .... costs.
- Prepare cost breakdown for the bank's (6) .... Manager.
- Meet Matt at (7) ....
- Remember report on (8) ....

What could go before the word 'manager'?

How could you finish the sentence 'Meet me at …'?

Check your answers on page 79. The recording scripts are on page 80.

Now do the test on pages 14–15.

Listening Test 🎧14

Part Two
Questions 11–22

- You will hear three conversations.
- Fill in the numbered spaces, using the information you hear.
- You will hear each conversation **once** only.

Conversation One
Questions 11–14

- Look at the form below.
- You will hear a phone call from a magazine reader to the magazine asking for franchising company prospectuses.

<u>Franchiser Magazine</u>

<u>Company Prospectus Request Form</u>

<u>Reader</u>

Name: Bill Tyson

Postcode: SN2 8BY

House number: 10

Current Position: (**11**) ....

Special skills/Qualifications: (**12**) ....

<u>Franchise company prospectus request</u>:

Type of company interested in: (**13**) ....

Geographical area of interest: (**14**) ....

Conversation Two
Questions 15–18

- Look at the message below.
- You will hear a phone message from a supply company.

Phone Message

For: Emily Chung

From: Sam Webster, SW Packaging Supplies

Re: your order for (**15**) .... rolls

The order delivery will be delayed until (**16**) .... –
they're waiting for an overdue (**17**) .... to arrive
from the manufacturers.

They apologise for the inconvenience. If this causes any problems, contact
(**18**) .... department on 01424 797999.

Conversation Three
Questions 19–22

- Look at the notes below.
- You will hear a phone call between an employment agent and his client about a
  job vacancy.

Vacant post: (**19**) .... at Campbell and Ross

Type of business: (**20**) ....

Additions to basic salary: (**21**) .... , pension and long holidays

Closing date for applications: (**22**) ....

Check your answers on page 80. The recording scripts are on pages 80–81.

Listening Part 3
Understanding short extracts (10 QUESTIONS)

This unit will help you to prepare for Part 3 of the Listening Test. This part of the test has 2 sections.

In each section:

- you will hear 5 people talking
- the 5 people might be talking about 5 different subjects or about different parts of the same subject
- you have to decide what subject, or part of the subject, each person is talking about
- you have 9 options to choose from (A–I)

Points to remember

- This part of the test checks how well you can understand what a speaker means (what his or her main message is). It does not test how well you can understand individual words or numbers like Part 1 or Part 2.
- You will only hear each recording once, so be prepared for this.
- You will have 20 seconds to look at each part before you listen. Use this time carefully. Read the question and think about what type of language or vocabulary you might hear for each part.
- There is an example at the beginning of each section. (The answer to this is always I.)

This is an example of what you will see in Part 3, Section 1 of the Listening Test:

Part Three
Section One
Questions 23–27

> *This bullet tells you what subject you will hear people talking about.*

> *This bullet tells you what to do in the test.*

- You will hear five people talking about the department of a company where they work.
- As you listen to each one, decide in what part of their company each person works.
- Choose your answer from the list **A–I**, and write the correct letter in the space provided.
- You will hear the five pieces **once** only.

Example: .... I ....

> *I is always the example.*

Listening skills practice

In this section, you are going to practise listening skills for Part 3 questions.

Look back at the example of a question in Part 3, Section 1 of the Listening Test. Then look at the recording script below for the example. Which department is the person talking about?

A	delivery department
B	customer services
C	sales and marketing
D	accounts department
E	research and development
F	quality control
G	production department
H	IT department
I	training department

> *Remember: this is always the example.*

Example

We get a lot of people straight from university and the problem is, they may have studied business and know something about finance[1] and cash flow[2] and things like that, but not how to run a meeting or what to do if customers complain[3]. That's what we do – we turn them from students into managers.

1, 2 and 3 are included to distract you. You hear words which sound like they might be one of the answers. 'Finance' and 'cash flow' could be connected to the accounts department (D). 'Customers complain' could be connected to customer services (B). In this example, they are not the correct answer.

> *This is talking about teaching staff new skills, so you write I – training department.*

Look at the recording scripts below and listen to speakers 1 and 2.

The first time you listen:
- **complete the spaces in the recording scripts. These words are distractors (words or expressions that sound like possible answers, but in fact are not).**
- **then in the left-hand column, write the letter of the department name (and the department name) that the distractor in each space refers to.**

> **A**   delivery department
> **B**   customer services
> **C**   sales and marketing
> **D**   accounts department
> **E**   research and development
> **F**   quality control
> **G**   production department
> **H**   IT department
> **I**   training department

The second time you listen:
- **underline the correct answer in the recording scripts and write the answers in the spaces provided.**

🎧 15

Space 1 ......*G*......

...*production*.... department

Space 2 ....

.... department

Person 1: I know we're working hard to increase (**1**) ....*output*...... and improve (**2**) .... , but it doesn't really matter how good our products are, or how many we make, if the customers aren't interested in buying them. We make sure that customers know our products exist, see them in magazines and newspapers, and so on.

Answer: .... (.................... department)

> *Which department was this person talking about? Write the letter and the department name here.*

🎧 16

Space 3 ....

.... department

Space 4 ....

.... department

Person 2: We don't get that many (**3**) .... these days, but when we do, it's probably my responsibility. If a customer receives one of our products that doesn't work, OK I didn't (**4**) .... it myself, but I, or someone in my department should have noticed the problem before it left the factory; it should have been checked.

Answer: .... (.................... department)

Check your answers on page 81. The recording scripts are also are on page 81.

Test practice

🎧 17 Now listen to speakers 3, 4 and 5 and choose the correct letter for each one.

Person 3   ....

Person 4   ....

Person 5   ....

Check your answers on page 81. The recording scripts are also on page 81.

Now do the test on page 18.

Listening Test 🎧18

Part Three
Section One
Questions 23–27

- You will hear five people talking about changes that companies have made.
- As you listen to each one, decide the area in which each company has made changes.
- Choose your answer from the list **A–I**, and write the correct letter in the space provided.
- You will hear the five pieces **once** only.

Example: ....I.........

23	Person 1	....
24	Person 2	....
25	Person 3	....
26	Person 4	....
27	Person 5	....

A	media exposure
B	product development
C	brand stretching
D	group structure
E	workforce diversity
F	quality control
G	internal communication channels
H	customer loyalty
I	organisation of work activities

Section Two
Questions 28–32

- You will hear five people giving advice about what to do before signing a contract.
- As you listen to each one, decide what advice each speaker gives.
- Choose your answer from the list **A–I**, and write the correct letter in the space provided.
- You will hear the five pieces **once** only.

Example: ....I.........

28	Person 1	....
29	Person 2	....
30	Person 3	....
31	Person 4	....
32	Person 5	....

A	Be clear about what you want from the contract before reading it.
B	Make notes to summarise each section.
C	Always ask for changes if necessary.
D	While you read the contract, give it your full attention.
E	Be prepared to be flexible.
F	Never sign if you feel under pressure.
G	Ask another person to read it for you carefully.
H	Read each section of the contract more than once.
I	Always check the contracts written by your own lawyers.

Check your answers on page 81. The recording scripts are on pages 81–82.

Listening Part 4
Understanding a longer recording (18 QUESTIONS)

This unit will help you to prepare for Part 4 of the Listening Test. This part of the test has 3 sections: normally the easier questions are at the beginning.

There are 3 possible types of listening in this part:

- a monologue (1 person speaking)
- an interview (a dialogue where 1 person asks short questions and the other person answers)
- a conversation (a dialogue where both people talk for about the same amount of time)

You might hear:

- radio broadcasts
- speeches (e.g. at conferences, presentations)
- meetings, job interviews and other business situations

Points to remember
- This part of the test checks how well you can understand details, attitudes or opinions from a longer listening.
- You will hear each recording twice, so you have a chance to check your answers the second time you listen and even to change your answer if you think it is wrong.
- The questions are multiple choice (A, B or C) so only 1 answer can be correct.
- Never leave a question unanswered. If you don't know, guess! (You have a 1 in 3 chance of being correct.)
- Remember that the words used will not be the same in the question and the options (A, B or C) as in the listening text. You need to listen for words/expressions with similar meanings.
- You will have 20 seconds to look at each part before you listen. Use this time carefully to read the question and the 3 options. Think about the information you need to find. Underline the key word(s) in the question.

This is an example of what you will see in Part 4, Section 1 of the Listening Test:

> You can find out 3 important details here:
> 1 the type of listening text
> 2 who is speaking (and how many people there are)
> 3 what they are talking about

Part Four
Section One
Questions 33–38

- You will hear a radio interview[1] with Jane Holden, a Human Resources specialist[2], talking about problems with recruiting new staff[3].
- For questions **33–38**, circle **one** letter A, B or C for the correct answer.
- You will hear the conversation **twice**.

33 According to Jane, what is the biggest problem companies have when recruiting new staff?
   A There aren't enough qualified people available.
   B Most people don't have the right experience.
   C Training doesn't attract young people.

> In the text you probably won't hear exactly the same questions when you listen so it's important to listen for similar words.

> This is an important word. It tells you what type of problem to listen for.

This is what you will hear:

Interviewer: Jane, what is the <u>biggest</u> problem companies have when looking for new staff these days?

Jane: <u>We're still having a few problems finding people with the right qualifications and experience</u>. Those problems will always exist, but one thing we now see – and I think this is very serious – is that <u>school leavers just aren't interested in training – perhaps it's the low salaries</u>.

> Does 'a few' mean these problems are very serious?

> Does this look like any of the options A, B or C?

The correct answer is C.

Listening skills practice

19 Look at the 4 questions from an interview with a businessman, but cover the options (A, B and C) for each one. Listen to excerpts from the interview and try to answer the questions without looking at the options.

1 When did Paul have his first real business experience?

   A after university
   B before university
   C during university

2 He got his first management job because

   A he was headhunted.
   B he knew someone at the company.
   C he had studied business.

3 What is some useful business advice Paul has had?

   A talk to your colleagues
   B think about customers' needs
   C keep costs low

4 According to Paul, the most important quality of a leader is

   A being prepared to listen to your team.
   B being prepared to make decisions.
   C being prepared to change your mind.

Now listen again, and look at both the options and the questions. Which one is correct?

Check your answers on page 82. The recording scripts are on pages 82–83.

Test practice

20 Now try this exercise. It is like the one you will see in the test. You will hear an extract from a presentation made by a woman about her company's services. This time read the questions and the options before you listen.

1 What does this company do?
   A help companies do business abroad
   B offer financial help to companies
   C give training to foreign workers

2 A franchise is a good idea because
   A your partner takes all the risk.
   B the costs are low.
   C they are very profitable.

3 How can this company help you with franchises?
   A They can help with contracts.
   B They help with the legal costs.
   C They find suitable partners.

4 What is the disadvantage of joint ventures?
   A They cost 50% more than a franchise.
   B They always take a long time to organise.
   C They can be ended by one partner.

Check your answers on page 82. The recording scripts are on pages 82–83.

Which method worked best for you: covering the options or reading them first? Use the method you liked best in the test.

Now do the test on pages 21–23.

Listening Test 🎧21

Part Four
Section One
Questions 33–38

- You will hear a college lecturer talking about the contribution of production and marketing to achieving business aims.
- For questions **33–38**, circle **one** letter **A**, **B** or **C** for the correct answer.
- You will hear the talk **twice**.

33 According to the speaker, in mass production decision-making is

   A   based on workers' skills.

   B   separate from production itself.

   C   a continuous process.

34 In the shoe factory, the 'walk' was a term used to describe

   A   the distance materials had to be moved in production.

   B   how much time it took to move shoes through production.

   C   how far each worker needed to move during production.

35 The production manager was surprised because

   A   quality was improved.

   B   efficiency was increased.

   C   space was saved.

36 What was a sign of success for the car factory?

   A   Errors were less likely to be serious.

   B   Fewer suppliers were needed.

   C   The amount of stock was reduced.

37 The ice cream company decided to focus their competitiveness on

   A   making sure that their prices undercut those of their rivals.

   B   ensuring that their products were consistently of high quality.

   C   setting up an effective distribution network.

38 The ice cream company's marketing strategy was special because they

   A   introduced the product in a new kind of packaging.

   B   advertised the product more widely than their competitors.

   C   depended on customers telling each other about the product.

Section Two
Questions 39–44

- You will hear a radio interview with Simon Cartier, the owner of a chain of clothing shops.
- For questions **39–44**, circle **one** letter **A**, **B** or **C** for the correct answer.
- You will hear the interview **twice**.

39 Why did Cartier leave the company that employed him for ten years?

    A   He was replaced by a new appointee.

    B   His position disappeared in a restructuring of the company.

    C   The company was closed down.

40 To start his first business, *The Outfit*, he used

    A   venture capitalists.

    B   his own savings.

    C   money from Jack Cartier.

41 What section of the clothing market was his second company, *Massive Stores,* aimed at?

    A   clothing for a specialist market

    B   top-of-the-range clothing for leisure

    C   reduced price clothing

42 What advantage did previous experience in business give him when developing *Massive Stores*?

    A   He knew who to turn to for advice on starting the business.

    B   Manufacturers were willing to take a risk by helping him.

    C   A landlord let him have premises at a reduced rent.

43 Which area of business does he concentrate on now?

    A   the overall management of the company's finances

    B   the control of purchasing of stock for retailing

    C   the setting up of additional outlets

44 How does he feel about the possibility of retiring from business?

    A   He enjoys the world of business too much to give it up.

    B   He looks forward to spending more time doing leisure activities.

    C   He'd like to take temporary retirement for a while then return to work.

Section Three
Questions 45–50

- You will hear Diana Warren, a business consultant, giving a talk on how she set up her business consultancy.
- For questions **45–50**, circle **one** letter **A**, **B** or **C** for the correct answer.
- You will hear the talk **twice**.

45 What was the first step Diana Warren took when she decided to be a business consultant?

    A   She identified the areas where there was a lack of specialists.

    B   She examined what her career had taught her.

    C   She took time to research potential clients.

46 What does she say about her own personal qualities?

    A   She had to pretend to be confident when she started her consultancy.

    B   She believes experience gave her sufficient confidence.

    C   She has always had plenty of confidence with clients.

47 She says the skills that you offer as a consultant ideally ought to suit clients

    A   in areas where demand is growing.

    B   in areas likely to emerge in the future.

    C   in an area which has maintained its popularity.

48 To sell your 'product', she says you need to

    A   promote as many of your skills as possible.

    B   list particular skills that you can provide.

    C   present your skills in clear groups.

49 How did she market her new consultancy?

    A   She advertised in industry publications.

    B   She asked her first clients to recommend her.

    C   She informed all the people she knew about it.

50 What is her opinion about writing articles for business journals?

    A   It was time-consuming, but provided useful publicity.

    B   The articles brought in a lot of new business in a short time.

    C   Writing for internet sites was a more profitable use of her time.

Check your answers on page 83. The recording scripts are on pages 83–85.

The BULATS Reading and Language Knowledge Test

The BULATS Reading and Language Knowledge Test takes 60 minutes. You must also write your answers on a separate Answer Sheet during this time. You can see an example of an Answer Sheet on page 95.

The aim of this part is to test your skills in reading and your knowledge of grammar and vocabulary.

The Reading and Language Knowledge Test is divided into 2 parts. In general, the second part is more difficult than the first part.

Part 1

There are 4 sections in this part of the test (24 questions in total):

You will read	Your task	Test focus
1 7 short texts	• 7 multiple-choice questions • 3 options for each question (A, B or C)	understanding notices, messages, adverts, timetables, etc.
2 6 sentences about different topics	• complete 6 spaces • 4 options for each space (A, B, C or D)	grammar and vocabulary
3 a text on a business topic (300–400 words), usually a newspaper story, magazine article, advertisement, brochure, leaflet or report	• 6 multiple-choice questions • 3 options for each question (A, B or C)	understanding the general meaning and details of a text
4 a text about a business topic (75–150 words)	• complete 5 spaces with 1 word	grammar

Part 2

There are 6 sections in this part of the test (36 questions in total):

You will read	Your task	Test focus
1 4 different texts about a similar topic	• match 7 sentences to the texts	understanding details of a text
2 a text about a business topic (75–150 words)	• complete 5 spaces • 4 options for each space (A, B, C or D)	grammar and vocabulary
3 a text about a business topic (75–150 words)	• complete 5 spaces with 1 word	grammar
4 6 sentences about different business topics	• complete 6 spaces • 4 options for each space (A, B, C or D)	grammar and vocabulary
5 a long text about a business topic (450–550 words), usually a newspaper or magazine article, report, advertisement or leaflet	• 6 multiple-choice questions • 4 options for each question (A, B, C or D)	understanding the general meaning and details of a text (including opinions)
6 a text about a business topic (100–150 words), usually a letter, memo, email or advertisement	• find and correct 7 mistakes	grammar and vocabulary

The preparation you do for Part 1 will also help you with Part 2. This is because some of the tasks in Part 2 are the same as the ones in Part 1, but the questions in Part 2 are generally more difficult.

Reading and Language Knowledge Part 1, Section 1
Understanding notices and short extracts (7 QUESTIONS)

This unit will help you to prepare for Part 1, Section 1 of the Reading and Language Knowledge Test. In this part of the test, you read 7 short texts and choose the correct answer from 3 options.

You might read:

- notices
- signs
- messages
- advertisements
- timetables
- brochures
- leaflets
- graphs

Points to remember

- This part of the test checks your understanding of 'survival' English in the workplace.
- The questions are multiple choice (A, B or C) so only 1 answer can be correct.
- Read the text and the options (A, B and C), then underline the key words.
- When you have finished, check your answers. Think about why the other 2 options are incorrect.

Part One
Section One
Questions 51–57

- Look at the following messages and notices.
- For questions **51–57**, mark **one** letter **A**, **B** or **C** on your Answer Sheet.

These are the key words in the message.

Example

See attached price list for details of our special offers.

You do not need to contact the company.

A You should contact this company for details of their special offers.

B You can find out more about special offers by looking at a separate document.

C You will find more information on special offers on another page.

The price list is not separate, it is attached.

The correct answer is C.

Practice exercises
Synonyms

Recognising words or expressions with the same or similar meanings can be very helpful in this type of test because it can help you to eliminate incorrect options.

Match the sentences 1–5 with a sentence with the same meaning a–e.

1 I apologise for calling off our meeting at such short notice. ..e..

2 We regret to inform you that the product you ordered is no longer in stock. ......

3 This company is second-to-none in its field of business. ......

4 All enquiries should be directed to the relevant department. ......

5 I will be away from the office all day tomorrow. Back on Friday. ......

a I am sorry to tell you that it is unavailable at the present time.

b I won't be at my desk until the end of the week.

c Please pass on any questions to the correct office.

d We have the best reputation in our line of business.

e We'll have to cancel our appointment, I'm afraid. Something's come up at the last minute.

Identifying why a person is writing

You might have to identify why someone is writing a particular text.

Match the expressions from the list a–l with the reasons for writing 1–6. There are 2 answers for each reason.

1 Providing explanations ..d.. ......

2 Offering to do something ....

3 Requesting something ....

4 Informing someone ....

5 Complaining about something ....

6 Enquiring about something ....

a I am pleased to tell you that your order is ready.

b I'm afraid this is not acceptable.

c I would be grateful if you could send me a copy.

d The late arrival was the result of a train strike.

e If we can help you in any way, please do not hesitate to ask.

f I'd really appreciate it if you sent me a new price list.

g Due to a problem with our supplier, all deliveries will be delayed.

h I'm writing to ask you when it will be ready for collection.

i I have to advise you that your payment is late.

j I am extremely dissatisfied with the product I bought.

k Could you let me know how often you deliver?

l We would be delighted to discuss this in more detail.

Check your answers on page 85.

Test practice

Now try these questions. They are like the ones you will see in the test.

Choose the correct option (A, B or C).

1 The Central Plaza Hotel offers Toronto's biggest fully-equipped business centre for meetings, conventions and other business needs. Ideal for the business traveller.

Why would you choose this hotel?

The Central Plaza

A offers the best facilities for business guests in Toronto.

B is only recommended for business people.

C would suit large companies wishing to hold a conference.

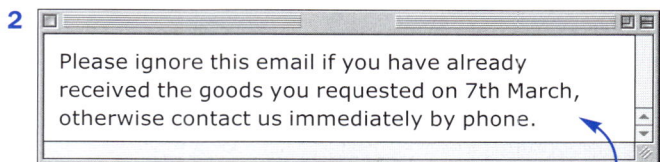

2

Please ignore this email if you have already received the goods you requested on 7th March, otherwise contact us immediately by phone.

What does this email tell you?

Can you explain this in your own words before you look at the options?

A You need to telephone the company to tell them if your order has arrived.

B You don't need to reply to this email if your order has been delivered.

C You should email the company if you want to arrange a new delivery date.

3 To qualify for a 10% discount, your order must exceed $5,000. We cannot make an exception, even for new customers.

What are the key words in this message?

What is this company's policy on discounts?

A All new customers get a 10% discount on their orders.

B No customers can get a discount on orders of less than $5,000.

C New customers have to spend more than $5,000 on their first order.

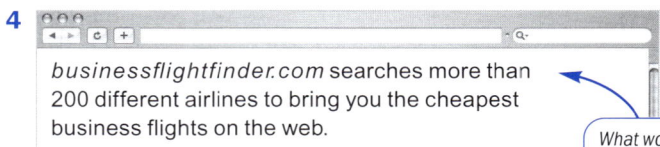

4

businessflightfinder.com searches more than 200 different airlines to bring you the cheapest business flights on the web.

What would you expect to buy from this company?

businessflightfinder.com is

A an agency for budget business travel.

B a low-cost business airline.

C an online guide to using the internet for travel.

Check your answers on page 85.

Now do the test on pages 28–30.

Reading and Language Knowledge Test

Part One
Section One
Questions 51–57

- Look at the following messages and notices.
- For questions **51–57**, mark **one** letter **A**, **B** or **C** on your Answer Sheet.

Example:

STORE CONTENTS IN A COOL PLACE OUT OF DIRECT SUNLIGHT

A The contents should be kept at a constant temperature.

B The contents are sensitive to heat and light.

C The contents must be kept frozen.

0	A	B	C
	⬜	⬛	⬜

51

> Order reference 122/HB
>
> We regret to advise you that the despatch date for the above will now be later than you were originally informed, and we now anticipate despatching your order at the beginning of November.

What is the purpose of this letter?

A to apologise for being unable to supply the customer's order in November

B to answer a customer's complaint about the lateness of an order

C to notify the customer of a delay in sending an order

52

> Established in 1986, Martin and Co. let and manage flats and houses on behalf of landlord clients.

Martin and Co. operate as

A agents for those who own rented properties.

B sales representatives for those who want to buy properties to rent.

C consultants for those who want to set up in the property business.

53

> You have received this promotional email because you have agreed to receive VAL Products marketing information. To reverse this, log onto your personal account page at www.VAL.com.

You should go to your account page at the website to

A cancel an agreement to be sent publicity mail.

B find out more about the promotion.

C give your opinion on their latest campaign.

54

> Our free, no-ties price comparison service finds the cheapest prices from hundreds of retailers for thousands and thousands of office products.

This is an advertisement for

A a supplier of low cost office products.

B a consumer guide to costs for office products.

C a directory of office products available from different outlets.

55

> BHJ Group Industries
> Key priorities for the year ahead
> - Drive profit recovery in the Middle East
> - Make profit for the first time in Central Europe
> - Establish most profitable brands in Africa

BHJ plan to give attention to regaining profits which have declined in

A the Middle East.

B Central Europe.

C Africa.

56

> *Jardine's has overhauled packaging across its 40-strong breakfast cereal, fruit bar and snack bar portfolio in an effort to create a single and more recognisable brand identity.*

Jardine's has changed its packaging so that consumers can more easily

A distinguish between different Jardine ranges.

B pick out Jardine's products.

C decide which Jardine product suits them best.

57

> A recent survey found that 26% of firms questioned had made incorrect IT purchasing decisions because they had been misled by the technical IT language used by the suppliers.

Firms bought the wrong IT products because they

A didn't use outlets which provided expert guidance.

B weren't knowledgeable enough about current products.

C hadn't been able to understand the sellers correctly.

Check your answers on page 85.

Reading and Language Knowledge Part 1, Section 2

Sentences with a gap (6 QUESTIONS)

This unit will help you to prepare for Part 1, Section 2 of the Reading and Language Knowledge Test. This part of BULATS tests your knowledge of grammar and vocabulary. In this part of the test, there are 6 questions. For each question you have to complete a sentence with the correct word. There are 4 options (A, B, C or D) for each question.

Points to remember
- If you answer a question, it will not help you with another one later. All questions are independent.
- Read the question carefully. Look at all the words which could help you in the question and in the options (A, B, C or D).
- You will also see this type of question in Part 2, Section 4, but in Part 2 the questions are generally more difficult.
- You must complete each sentence with 1 of the 4 options.
- Never leave a question unanswered. If you don't know, guess! (You have a 1 in 4 chance of being correct.)

Here is an example of a question from Part 1, Section 2 of the Reading and Language Knowledge Test:

Part One
Section Two
Questions 58–63
- Choose the word or phrase which best completes each sentence.
- For questions **58–63**, mark **one** letter **A**, **B**, **C** or **D** on your Answer Sheet.

58 This product has not been .... the market for long.
  A at
  B on
  C with
  D to

Which is correct, A, B, C or D? Check on page 85.

Keeping vocabulary records

Because the BULATS test can cover a wide range of vocabulary, it is important to keep good vocabulary records which will help you remember words and combinations of words.

Here are some suggestions for how to organise your vocabulary:

1 You could record collocations like this:

Company

Verbs: found, set up, run
Types: limited, private, public
Nouns: company director, company policy,
          company car

2 You could make notes on the grammar of a word:

Interested + in + verb-ing

His company was interested in expanding into the Asian market.

Some verbs in English are always used with a preposition (e.g. we apologise **to** someone **for** something). Verbs with prepositions are very common in this part of the test.

Tick (✓) the sentences where the prepositions are used correctly.

a I'm not happy. I would like to **complain about** this product I bought from you.

b This is a public company. It **belongs to** the shareholders.

c The management are **discussing about** this problem.

d The best products only **consist of** a few parts.

e I might accept your offer. It **depends on** the price.

f This type of product is **aimed at** young people.

g When will you **pay** me **by** the work I did last week?

h Time for questions is **included to** my presentation.

Check your answers on page 85.

3 You could record groups of words with the same or similar meaning:

> make
> create   build   construct   produce

Divide these verbs into three groups in the table.

> present acquire propose boost achieve further

obtain	offer	improve
....	....	....
....	....	....

Check your answers on page 86.

It is also a good idea to write example sentences to help you remember how to use new vocabulary.

> I obtained a copy of the report yesterday.
> He offered a lot of money for my company.
> The new machinery will help us to improve quality by 25%.

Complete the sentences with the correct form of the verbs in the table above.

a I'd like to ask each department to .... its annual budget to the board of directors on Monday.

b Our target is a turnover of $4m and we hope to .... it by the end of the year.

c The recent fall in oil prices has .... the economy significantly.

What tense is formed with 'have' + past participle?

d German cars have .... a reputation for reliability and quality.

e The new government .... to reduce taxes in April.

f He moved to the New York office to .... his career.

Check your answers on page 86.

Test practice

Now try these questions. They are like the ones you will see in the test.

Choose the word which best completes each sentence.

1 Our new pocket PC is targeted .... the business traveller.
  A at
  B on
  C with
  D to

'Targeted' is like 'aimed'. What preposition collocates with 'aimed'?

2 One of the .... to consumers of competition between companies is lower prices.
  A benefits
  B advances
  C improvements
  D profits

Which ones are definitely wrong?

3 People are .... less on luxury goods than they were last year.
  A buying
  B purchasing
  C paying
  D spending

The collocation here is with 'on'. Which verb follows this pattern?

4 The management are .... a possible pension plan for the employees.
  A discussing
  B talking
  C thinking
  D deciding

Which of these verbs does not need a preposition?

5 Our market .... is declining. We've got to do something.
  A proportion
  B section
  C portion
  D share

Which of these goes best with 'market'?

6 In my report I've .... the sales figures you asked for.
  A involved
  B contained
  C included
  D comprised

If you change the sentence to 'I've .... the sales figures in my report', does that help?

Check your answers on page 86.

Now do the test on page 33.

Reading and Language Knowledge Test

Part One
Section Two
Questions 58–63

- Choose the word or phrase which best completes each sentence.
- For questions **58–63**, mark **one** letter **A**, **B**, **C** or **D** on your Answer Sheet.

58 The packaging is aimed .... attracting teenage consumers.

   A   to

   B   at

   C   of

   D   on

59 They hope to .... their objective of €1 million in sales by December.

   A   complete

   B   achieve

   C   acquire

   D   obtain

60 Orders for delivery the same day should be placed no later .... 12.00 noon.

   A   but

   B   and

   C   as

   D   than

61 Anyone involved .... the recruitment process should be trained for it.

   A   in

   B   by

   C   for

   D   over

62 The supplier is .... some very competitive prices.

   A   presenting

   B   bidding

   C   handing

   D   offering

63 The landlord allowed him to pay rent in ....

   A   behind

   B   afterwards

   C   arrears

   D   debt

Check your answers on page 86.

Reading and Language Knowledge Part 1, Section 3

Longer text with multiple-choice questions (6 QUESTIONS)

This unit will help you to prepare for Part 1, Section 3 of the Reading and Language Knowledge Test. This part of BULATS tests your knowledge of longer pieces of writing. You read a text and answer 6 multiple-choice questions, choosing the correct answer from 3 options.

You might read:

- a newspaper or magazine article
- an advertisement
- a brochure, leaflet, or other company information
- a report

Points to remember

- The questions are always in the same order as the text. If you have a situation where this doesn't happen, you have missed an answer.
- The questions are always about facts in the text. Sometimes you have a question about opinions (e.g. What's the writer's main point in paragraph 1?), but the answer will be based on facts from the text.
- Usually there is 1 question per paragraph, but sometimes there are 2.
- If you answer a question, it will not help you with another one later. All questions are independent.
- Identify the key words (the most important words) in the text and in the options (A, B or C) and look for synonyms (words or expressions with the same or similar meaning). These can sometimes help you to identify the correct option.

Here is an example of a question from Part 1, Section 3 of the Reading and Language Knowledge Test:

Part One
Section Three
Questions 64–69

Read these instructions carefully. They tell you what you're reading (e.g. an article), and what it is about (e.g. fun in the workplace).

- Read the <u>article</u> below about <u>fun in the workplace</u> and answer questions **64–69** on the opposite page.
- For questions **64–69**, mark **one** letter **A**, **B** or **C** on your Answer Sheet.

Practice exercise

You are going to practise understanding what a text is about and what some of the language in it means.

Read the first paragraph of the text below and answer the question.

1 What do you think the text will be about?
  A how to increase profits
  B the benefits of enjoying work
  C improving relationships with colleagues

Check your answer on page 86.

Fun in the workplace

There is an idea that fun isn't appropriate in the workplace. However, the experience of increasing numbers of companies is that integrating fun and work together not only leads to better working relationships with our colleagues, but also makes more money for the company.

How can we make work fun? Changing attitudes doesn't happen overnight. Clear leadership from the management will help, but showing your staff you trust them is a vital first step. If you can trust your staff with your valuable customers, you should be able to trust them to work hard and still have fun.

One of the most successful ways of raising levels of fun in a company is recruiting one of the many people who enjoy life and love being sociable. Hire these people and then train them to do a job. This unusual approach might be difficult for some people to accept, but training people to have fun is almost impossible.

Finally, make an effort to recognise and applaud people's achievements. Many believe that money is the most effective motivator; in fact it is just one factor. Public praise is one of the most powerful ways to make people feel good about their jobs. Almost everyone enjoys the approval of their colleagues and friends. Don't you?

Read the rest of the text and answer these questions.

2 Look at these statements about paragraph 2. Are they true, false or not mentioned?

  A Making people think differently takes time.

  B Employees need to know their employers can rely on them.

  C Customers are more important than staff.

3 According to paragraph 3, are these statements true, false or not mentioned?

  A New staff usually enjoy their jobs more than experienced staff.

  B It's hard to find the right kind of new staff.

  C Teaching people to have fun at work is not easy.

4 Which of these ideas are mentioned in paragraph 4?

  A When someone does something well, you should congratulate them.

  B Financial rewards produce the best work.

  C Most people feel the same way when others say good things about them.

> Not all the wrong options (A, B or C) have distractors in the text, but they are written to seem believable.

Before you check your answers, do the vocabulary exercise below.

Vocabulary

Find words or expressions in the text on page 34 which mean the same as these definitions below.

Paragraph 1

  1 suitable or correct

  2 joining things together

  3 results in

Paragraph 2

  4 ways of thinking, feeling or behaving

  5 very important, necessary or essential

  6 useful or important

Paragraph 3

  7 increasing or improving

  8 enjoy the company of other people, friendly

  9 way of doing something

Paragraph 4

  10 show you think something is good or that you enjoy something

  11 an influence on a situation

  12 feel, show or say that something is good or that you agree with it

Check your answers on page 86, then look at the multiple-choice questions in the practice exercise again. Do you want to change any of your answers? Then check your answers on page 86.

Test practice

Now try these questions about the text on fun in the workplace on page 34. They are like the ones you will see in the test.

1 The author says that helping employees enjoy their jobs

  A improves salaries.

  B increases profits.

  C creates loyalty.

> Can you find all of these in paragraph 1?

2 In paragraph 2, what does the writer say is the best way to change attitudes?

  A to change the management of the company

  B to give people more responsibility

  C to demonstrate you have confidence in your staff

> What's another word for 'confidence' in paragraph 2?

3 If companies want to make working more enjoyable they should

  A start by improving the training programme.

  B hire the right kind of people.

  C find members of staff who can set a good example.

> One of these isn't mentioned in paragraph 3. Which one?

4 What is the writer's attitude to money in paragraph 4?

  A There are other ways of motivating people.

  B Most people are motivated by money more than anything.

  C People with money tend to have more friends.

> Do A and B mean the same thing?

Check your answers on page 86.

Now do the test on pages 36–37.

Reading and Language Knowledge Test

Part One
Section Three
Questions 64–69

- Read the article below about a company which makes use of direct marketing and answer questions **64–69** on the opposite page.
- For questions **64–69**, mark **one** letter **A**, **B** or **C** on your Answer Sheet.

<u>Dosh and Direct Marketing</u>

Dosh Software was set up by accountant Jonathan Van der Borgh to develop new accounting packages for financial services firms. Dosh was keen to get a retail presence, but was fighting for space on the shelves in big stores. They quickly realised that direct marketing would be a quicker and easier way to establish the brand. As a new company, explained Tony Trevillion, general manager, Dosh had to spend carefully. That is why direct marketing had so much appeal. Dosh could mail to discrete groups, targeting a customer base of accountants and book-keepers.

One of their first promotions, for example, was through an accountancy publication. Dosh placed an advertisement in the publication, which is distributed to 70,000 readers. In addition, they refined that list and placed a further 10,000 trial copies of their software on the cover of the publication but these were only to be received by smaller accountancy firms.

The results of each campaign are tracked and within just one or two weeks, the company will know how successful that mailing has been. After each campaign, phone calls are made to potential customers that responded as well as those that did not.

However, Dosh has learnt from some bad experiences and all of its marketing is costed against the expected return. 'If you buy a cold list, you will be lucky to get a return of half a per cent,' said Trevillion. Now that the group has been running for over two years and has built up its own database of customers, they are learning that this is the best list of all. 'It is always easier to sell to someone that you have sold to before,' said Trevillion. This has meant an investment in database technology to help Dosh keep up-to-date and accurate listings. But it was money well spent, according to Trevillion.

No opportunity is lost, and Dosh use every invoice mailing to make full use of the postal charges. As well as an invoice, customers could receive additional information about the company or questionnaires regarding customer service, all within the weight limit allowed for second-class mail. 'For me, as an accountant, the nice thing about direct marketing is that you can measure the success. You know all the costs – the creative costs, the mail, the time involved, the envelopes – and it is a very accurate measurement,' said Van der Borgh.

64 Why does Tony Trevillion say it was a good idea for Dosh to use direct marketing?

    A The accountant owner of Dosh had extensive customer lists.

    B The big retailers refused to stock Dosh software.

    C Their finances were more efficiently used targeting defined groups.

65 Who was intended to receive the free samples of Dosh products?

    A the 70,000 readers of an accountancy publication

    B members of smaller accountancy firms

    C accountants whose details Dosh found in advertisements

66 How does Dosh follow up direct marketing campaigns?

    A They chase responses for one to two weeks after the campaign.

    B They contact all the targets of the campaign.

    C They record details of just those who respond.

67 Why did Dosh have to purchase new database technology?

    A to record results of marketing campaigns

    B to replace unsuccessful customer lists

    C to keep track of current customers

68 What kind of money-saving scheme is detailed in the last paragraph?

    A They advertise other companies when they send invoices.

    B They enclose more of their literature with invoices.

    C They send out one invoice to cover several orders.

69 What does Van der Borgh say is the advantage of applying direct marketing as an accountant?

    A He is good at assessing how well a campaign has done.

    B He runs campaigns efficiently because he can foresee expenses.

    C He has a lot of experience of advising on marketing campaigns.

Check your answers on page 87.

Reading and Language Knowledge
Filling gaps in a text

The things most commonly tested are:

- articles
- *some*, *any*, etc.
- *this*, *that*, *these*, *those*
- tenses
- passives with *by*
- *-ing* or infinitive

- prepositions
- modal verbs
- linking words
- relative clauses
- phrasal verbs

Points to remember

- First, read the text very carefully.
- Think about what kind of word is missing. Is it a verb, a preposition or something else?
- Look at the words before and after the spaces.
- When you have finished, read the text to yourself again. If something sounds wrong to you, have another look at it.
- Fill in the spaces on the question paper first, but don't transfer your answers to the Answer Sheet until you are happy with them.

Here is an example of a question from Part 1, Section 4 of the Reading and Language Knowledge Test:

Part One
Section Four
Questions 70–74

- For questions **70–74**, read the text below and think of the word which best fits each space.
- Write only **one** word in each space on your Answer Sheet.

Don't write more than one word on your Answer Sheet.

Example:
She (**0**) .... born in Italy.

| 0 | was | ▭ ▭ |

Practice exercises

These exercises look at some of the most common areas tested in this part of the test.

Articles

Here is some information about articles:

Use **a**
- with countable nouns.
- when we mention countable nouns for the first time.
- when there is more than one of a countable noun (e.g. *I'd like a bottle of milk, please.* There is more than one bottle of milk in the shop).

Use **an** like **a** but usually before words starting with *a, e, i, o* or *u* (and before *h* in words where it is silent, e.g. *an hour*).

Use **the** with all types of noun
- when a noun is mentioned for the second time (e.g. *I have a laptop and a PC. I use the laptop on business trips*).
- with superlatives (e.g. *the longest*).
- when there is only one of something present (e.g. *The photocopier isn't working*) or in the world (e.g. *the President of France*).

There are some words that do not follow this rule, e.g. 'university', which starts with a /j/ sound like 'you'.

This is a countable noun and there is more than one manufacturer of equipment for oil companies.

Complete the text with *a*, *an* or *the*.

Priory Engineering Ltd is (**1**) .....*a*..... manufacturer of equipment for oil companies. (**2**) .... company was founded in 1948 and it is one of (**3**) .... biggest companies in its field. Priory has (**4**) .... workforce of 2,000 people.

One of its biggest projects is (**5**) .... underwater oil storage facility in the North Sea. Of course, (**6**) .... oil industry is not (**7**) .... only area where Priory is active. They also supply (**8**) .... American aircraft manufacturer with specialist engine parts and produce (**9**) .... range of products for construction companies.

Check your answers on page 87.

some, any, much, many, this, that, these, those

Complete the texts with the correct word for each space.

STAFF NOTICE

Are (**1**) .... members of staff interested in overtime work for the next two weeks? We have received a substantial order and need to complete it urgently. We will be able to say how (**2**) .... work will be available depending on how (**3**) .... people are interested. (**4**) .... employees who wish to apply for (**5**) .... work should see their supervisor immediately.

1	some	any	much
2	much	many	any
3	much	many	some
4	Those	That	This
5	those	this	these

A changing workforce

In the past, heavy industry needed large numbers of workers, but, as technology has developed, (**6**) .... days have gone. (**7**) .... people may lose their jobs as factories close, but (**8**) .... people are quickly finding new work in the rapidly expanding service sector. (**9**) .... sector now employs around 60% of the workforce and is as important as heavy industry was in the past.

6	that	these	those
7	Some	Any	Much
8	this	these	that
9	These	This	Those

Check your answers on page 87.

Test practice

Now try this exercise. It is like the one you will see in the test. Read the text and complete each space with 1 word.

Don't write more than 1 word on your Answer Sheet.

What word is used with the present perfect tense and a point in time in the past?

The Excellence Programme

The Excellence Programme was started eight years ago and (**1**) .... then has become one of the (**2**) .... successful and popular training programmes for managers working in the Human Resources sector. In five intensive days, you will learn about (**3**) .... latest ideas for managing yourself and your team. You will find out how people see you as a manager and how you can use (**4**) .... information to improve your performance.

All our courses are run (**5**) .... experienced, professional staff and we guarantee to make a difference.

Interested? Then call us today for more information.

Think about the rules for using articles.

What kind of word is 'latest'?

What information?

to be + verb + …? What kind of structure is this?

Check your answers on page 87.

Now do the test on page 40.

Reading and Language Knowledge Test

Part One
Section Four
Questions 70–74

- For questions **70–74**, read the text below and think of the word which best fits each space.
- Write only **one** word for each space on your Answer Sheet.

Example:

He is very interested (**0**) .... computers.

Answer:

0	in	⬜ ⬜

Dear Customer

We are writing to ask you to take part in Johnson's latest customer survey (**70**) .... that we can find out if you are happy with our service.

We'd also like your views on some new developments at Johnson's. The survey data is being recorded (**71**) .... NSB Research, an independent research agency. This will ensure that all data is passed on to Johnson's anonymously – Johnson's won't even know which customers (**72**) .... taken part in the survey.

The questions are all online, short and straightforward, and should only take about 15 minutes (**73**) .... total. All survey participants will (**74**) .... entered into a draw to win €1,000 of travel vouchers. The closing date for completion of the survey is 9th May. We look forward to hearing from you at *www.marketsearchers.com*.

Check your answers on page 87.

Reading and Language Knowledge Part 2, Section 1
Finding information in short texts (7 QUESTIONS)

This unit will help you to prepare for Part 2, Section 1 of the Reading and Language Knowledge Test. This part of BULATS tests how well you can find specific information by reading. In this part of the test, you read 4 texts A–D and then match 7 sentences to the texts.

Points to remember

- Identify the key words (the most important words) in the texts and in the options. These can help you to identify the correct option.
- If you see the same words in the text and in one of the options, be careful – the correct option will probably use synonyms (different words with a similar meaning).
- Underline the part of the text where the answer is. This will make it easier to check your answers later.
- If you can't find one of the answers, leave it until you have found the other answers. If there is a text without an answer, that is probably the missing answer.
- When you have finished, check your answers again before you complete the Answer Sheet. Think about why the other options are wrong.

Here is an example of a question from Part 2, Section 1 of the Reading and Language Knowledge Test:

Part Two
Section One
Questions 75–81

- Read the sentences below and the comments on the four pieces of technical equipment.
- Which text does each sentence **75–81** refer to?
- For each sentence, mark **one** letter **A**, **B**, **C** or **D** on your Answer Sheet.

All the texts will be mentioned, so there must be at least one A, B, C or D answer.

Practice exercises
Sentence matching

In this part of the test you will need to find language in the text which has the same meaning as the 7 sentences you are given. In this exercise, you will practise matching sentences with similar meanings.

Look at sentences 1–8 in which an advertising executive describes pieces of technical equipment she uses: a personal organiser, a laptop, a mobile phone and an MP3 player. Match sentences 1–8 with sentences a–h.

1 Basically it's just an electronic diary and address book; it doesn't really do as much as I'd like. ..b..

2 I don't know how I'd do my job without it. ......

3 You can use it to check emails while watching TV at home. ......

4 I ran out of space on the first one so I had to get the bigger version. ......

5 I probably don't use 90% of its features because it takes too long to read the instructions. ......

6 If people know you have a mobile phone, they assume you're always available. ......

7 I send a lot of text messages – especially when I'm in a meeting. ......

8 I could use this while I'm relaxing, but I don't have enough time. ......

Remember: in the test you will be looking for sections of the text which have a similar meaning to the sentences in the question.

a This is my second one.

b I need something more sophisticated.

c It's useful for communicating when I can't make a phone call.

d It can be difficult to have any privacy.

e I have to have this for my business.

f You don't need to go to the office to do your work.

g I could check email while watching TV at home – if I have the chance.

h I'm too busy to learn how to use it properly.

Check your answers on page 87.

Vocabulary: Modal verbs

Modal verbs often appear in this part of the test.

Look at sentences 1–8. They give someone's opinion of different products. Sentences a–h express the same ideas but using modal verbs. Match sentences 1–8 with sentences a–h.

1 I bought this product, but it isn't useful. ....*h*...

2 This product is vital in my work. ......

3 I want one of these products, but I haven't got one yet. ......

4 I don't own one of these products, but it would be a very good idea to buy one. ......

5 It's possible I'll buy one of these products. ......

6 It wasn't necessary for me to buy one of these products. ......

7 It's not possible for me to buy one of these products. ......

8 It isn't necessary for me to buy one of these products. ......

The different tenses should help you to find the answers.

The modal verbs are in bold here.

a I **might** buy this product.

b I **needn't have** bought this product.

c I **have to** have this product.

d I **should** buy this product.

e I **don't have to** buy this product.

f I**'d like** this product.

g I **can't** buy this product.

h I **didn't need** this product.

Check your answers on page 87.

Vocabulary: Useful expressions

This exercise will help you with some of the language used in the test practice exercise on the next page.

1 Match the words or expressions a–h with the definitions 1–8.

a (to) prefer   e features

b all-in-one   f (to) check

c (to) run out of   g overall

d (a) version (of something)   h (to) assume

1 to choose one thing instead of another thing

2 important parts of something

3 speaking generally about something

4 to finish your supply of something

5 to believe, think or expect something is true even when you have no facts to show this

6 to look at or inspect something carefully

7 something which has two or more different uses or functions

8 something which is based on something else, but with some different features

Check your answers on page 87.

2 Complete the sentences below with the words or expressions a–h.

1 One of the most important .... of this computer is that it only weighs 1 kg.

2 We are unable to deliver your product until next week as we have .... stock.

3 I haven't called to confirm, but I .... you'll be able to meet me at the usual time tomorrow.

4 Could you .... the times of trains to London? I have to be there by 10.00 tomorrow.

5 This is our new product. It's an .... pen, torch and USB memory stick.

6 The product was launched last month and already there are plans for a new .... with more memory.

7 Of course there are some problems living outside the city – it takes longer to get to work for example – but, ... , I think the quality of life is better.

8 These days most people .... to buy a new computer than to have the old one repaired when there is a problem.

Check your answers on page 87.

Test practice

Now try this exercise. It is like the one you will see in the test.

In this exercise you are going to answer questions on the same topic you looked at in the sentence matching exercise on page 41 (an advertising executive describes pieces of technical equipment she uses).

Which text does each sentence refer to? Write one letter A, B, C or D in the space.

Example: She keeps buying new versions of this device.

Answer:

0	A	B	C	D

> There is always an example like this at the beginning of the test.

> Underline the key words in each sentence and then look for similar expressions in the texts.

1 This device helps in <u>many situations</u>. ......

2 This device makes it easier to relax. ......

> What's another word for 'relax'?

3 The owner has found these devices a little disappointing so far. ......

> Has she only owned one of these, or more than one?

4 She doesn't really enjoy owning this device. ......

> How would she probably feel without one?

5 She'd like one of these that had more functions.

......

> What do you call something with more than one function?

6 This device suits her lifestyle. ......

> What kind of lifestyle does she have?

> Have you got an A, B, C and D answer?

A Personal organiser

> Underline where the answers are in the texts. This is the example.

<u>I've had three of these already</u>, but none have been as good as I'd hoped. Basically it's just an electronic diary and address book; it's better than paper, but it doesn't really do as much as I'd like. What I'd prefer is an all-in-one version of this so I could use it to make phone calls, send emails and have internet access too.

B Laptop

Although I don't use all the features, I think it's the most useful thing I own. It has wireless internet access, so you can use it to check emails while watching TV at home – if I had the chance! As I said, I probably don't use 90% of its features because it takes too long to read the instructions, but I don't know how I'd do my job without it.

C Mobile phone

In my business I send a lot of text messages – especially when I'm in a meeting and a mobile is great for that, but overall though, I'd be happier without one of these. Of course they are useful, but if people know you have a mobile phone, they assume you're always available.

D MP3 player

This is important to me because music helps me unwind when I'm travelling, and I do a lot of travelling. I'm currently putting all my CD collection onto this. I <u>ran out of space</u> on the first one so I had to get the bigger version.

> Are there any good expressions to underline here?

Check your answers on page 87.

Now do the test on pages 44–45.

Reading and Language Knowledge Test

Part Two
Section One
Questions 75–81

- Read the sentences below and the comments that four different men make about their experience of franchising.
- Which text does each sentence **75–81** refer to?
- For each sentence, mark **one** letter **A**, **B**, **C** or **D** on your Answer Sheet.

Example:

0 He chose the company after investigating several other franchises.

Answer:

0	A	B	C	D
	■	▭	▭	▭

75 He first considered franchising when his employer went out of business.

76 He chose to buy the franchise because he thought it could be developed readily.

77 The franchising company has an established reputation.

78 He says he enjoys being his own boss for the first time.

79 He doesn't have to go looking for new business.

80 He wanted to buy a franchise which would be inexpensive to run and would earn him money straightaway.

81 His franchise company offers a range of ongoing business support services.

A

It was the promptness and professionalism of *Worksnax* that attracted me after I'd spent a lot of time researching various companies. I was seeking a business with low overheads, which would provide an income from the first week. My first call to their head office convinced me that these were the people I was looking for.

B

I'd always toyed with the idea of running my own business, and when rumours of redundancies emerged at work, I started looking seriously into the possibilities. By the time I had to leave, I'd chosen to invest in *The Home Agency* because it provided me with the opportunity to trade under a national and respected brand name. I was also able to benefit from their provision of tried and tested operating procedures, and from having a technical helpline and legal advice readily available once I was trading.

C

I had been a manager for McDonald's, another franchise company, but was attracted by the excellent growth potential and entry cost of *Lee Masons*. Also, I knew that I would be able to concentrate on what I've always enjoyed – managing the business and organising my 100+ staff, thanks to their nationwide team of sales professionals who find customers for all the franchises.

D

I was inspired by redundancy, when the company I'd been with for 23 years closed. I welcomed the new challenges of being self-employed, as I like working hard and relish the independence it gives me. The *Food Machine* franchise stood out because it was such an easy system to learn. Excellent training before I opened prepared me for most aspects of the business, including bookkeeping and marketing.

Check your answers on page 88.

Reading and Language Knowledge Part 2, Section 2

Filling gaps in a text (5 QUESTIONS)

This unit will help you to prepare for Part 2, Section 2 of the Reading and Language Knowledge Test. This part of BULATS tests grammar and vocabulary. You read a text (75–150 words) with 5 words missing. You have a choice of 4 words for each space.

> **Points to remember**
> - The text can be of any type of business writing (e.g. factual or descriptive) so reading business magazines and newspapers is very good preparation.
> - There are no questions on what the text is about. You only have to choose the correct missing word.
> - When you have finished, read your answers again. Look carefully at the words both before and after the space. When you are sure of your answer, write it on your Answer Sheet.

Here is an example of a question from Part 2, Section 2 of the Reading and Language Knowledge Test:

> **Part Two**
> **Section Two**
> **Questions 82–86**
>
> *Read these carefully. They tell you what the text is about.*
>
> - Read this article about buying a computer.
> - Choose the best word to fill each space from the words below.
> - For each question **82–86**, mark **one** letter **A**, **B**, **C** or **D** on your Answer Sheet.
>
> *Important!*

Practice exercises

Collocations

A collocation is a combination of two or more words which are frequently used together. This can be one way to identify the correct option for the missing words in this section. Look at the example below:

> Buying the new factory is the biggest investment the company has ever **made/done**.

The correct option is *made* because *investment* collocates with the verb *make* (*to do an investment* would be incorrect). An example of a collocation with *to do* is to *do business*, e.g. *We're interested in doing business with you.*

Choose the correct collocations.

The word that this collocates with could be before or after the space.

1 The decision has not been .... yet.
   A taken   **B** applied   **C** employed   **D** started

2 After several months of falling profits, they finally .... the need for changes.
   A believed   **B** consented   **C** accepted   **D** tolerated

3 This takeover will .... strengthen our position in the market.
   A more   **B** further   **C** added   **D** extra

4 To be eligible for the share scheme, you must .... several conditions.
   A please   **B** satisfy   **C** suit   **D** fit

5 Negotiations broke down when no agreement could be reached over the supplier's .... terms.
   A delivery   **B** arrival   **C** sending   **D** transfer

Check your answers on page 88.

Vocabulary

This exercise will help you with the test practice on this page.

Look at the words in the boxes and choose the best word to fill the space in each sentence below the boxes.

A result	**B** impact	**C** influence	**D** effect

1 We hope the advertising campaign will
...... *result* .... in a 20% increase in sales.

2 The first manager I worked for was the biggest
.... on my own management style.

A cost	**B** rate	**C** fee	**D** expenditure

3 The .... of inflation has risen for the third month in a row.

4 The government plans to increase
.... on health care.

A take up	**B** take part	**C** benefit	**D** advantage

5 Our shareholders will .... greatly from the takeover.

6 The unions and management will
.... in pay negotiations next week.

A established	**B** shown	**C** proved	**D** revealed

7 This company has .... our competitors that we are still the number one in the market.

8 Details of the secret merger were
.... at a press conference yesterday.

A size	**B** sum	**C** majority	**D** quantity

9 This project cost the firm a huge ....
of money.

10 If you buy a sufficient .... of goods, we will give you a 15% discount.

Check your answers on page 88.

Test practice

Now try this exercise. It is like the one you will see in the test. Read this article about a new government initiative and choose the best word to fill each space from the words below.

Remember to look before and after the spaces to help you choose your answer.

Does the preposition 'on' help you?

The Home Computer Initiative (HCI)

It is well known that happy, motivated staff are more productive, less likely to be absent and make a greater **(1)** .... on the workplace. These facts have inspired the Home Computer Initiative, an incentive scheme supported by the government, which aims to make it easier for companies to achieve real improvements in those areas at no **(2)** .... to the company.

The HCI offers a £500 tax exemption on computer equipment loaned out to employees at home. More and more companies are taking **(3)** .... of the scheme, which has, so far, **(4)** .... to be very successful. In the vast **(5)** .... of cases, the feedback, from both staff and customers, has been extremely positive. The government plans to expand the scheme next year.

Cross out any options you know are wrong.

1 A result	**B** impact	**C** influence	**D** ~~effect~~
2 A cost	**B** rate	**C** fee	**D** expenditure
3 A up	**B** part	**C** benefit	**D** advantage
4 A established	**B** shown	**C** proved	**D** revealed
5 A sum	**B** size	**C** majority	**D** quantity

Check your answers on page 88.

Now do the test on page 48.

Reading and Language Knowledge Test

Part Two
Section Two
Questions 82–86

- Read this text about the winner of a company award.
- Choose the best word to fill each space from the words below.
- For each question **82–86**, mark **one** letter **A**, **B**, **C** or **D** on your Answer Sheet.

Example:

He wants you to (**0**) .... him the reason.

0   **A** speak   **B** tell   **C** say   **D** talk

Answer:

0	A	B	C	D
	⬚	▬	⬚	⬚

Organisational Strength – The Shareplus Global Team

The Group President's Awards are presented to teams which have made an outstanding (**82**) .... to the group's strong results. The Shareplus Global Team wins the award for organisational strength. This team achieved a global first for MK Industries by (**83**) .... the first American-style employee share plan outside North America.

The team, led by Jane Barrymore and Rob Norwood, gained a full understanding of the local tax laws for each European country, (**84**) .... up a proposal for the plan and prepared communication materials in local languages for MK employees in the eligible countries. And all in just seven months!

The Shareplus plan was (**85**) .... across eight countries in Europe, giving more than 7,000 employees the opportunity to invest in the company. Nearly 20% of employees started (**86**) .... in the scheme within the first month of operation.

---

82 A addition   **B** payment   **C** contribution   **D** donation

83 A committing   **B** implementing   **C** performing   **D** engaging

84 A drew   **B** rose   **C** grew   **D** made

85 A opened   **B** originated   **C** founded   **D** launched

86 A involving   **B** participating   **C** including   **D** associating

Check your answers on page 88.

Reading and Language Knowledge Part 2, Section 3

Filling in gaps in a text (5 QUESTIONS)

This unit will help you to prepare for Part 2, Section 3 of the Reading and Language Knowledge Test. This part of BULATS tests grammar. You also saw this type of question in Part 1, Section 4, but in this part the questions are generally more difficult.

Practice exercises

These practice exercises will help you with some of the most typical language you will find in this part of the test.

which, that, who, where, when

Complete the definitions below.

a   We use ......*where*...... to talk about places.

b   We use .... to talk about people.

c   We use .... to talk about times.

d   We use .... or .... to talk about things.

> But be careful. Don't use 'that' after a comma (,) .

Now complete the text.

How he made his millions: Tom Bennett

One of Scotland's richest men,
(**1**) .... is worth around £500m, started his career in shoes.

> Is this referring to a thing or a time?

(**2**) .... most of his friends were beginning university, Tom was investing £5,000 in his first shop. Within five years he had opened the first of his chain of sports superstores, (**3**) .... he later sold for £290m. Bennett now invests in the property market, an area of business (**4**) .... growth has been huge.

> Is this referring to something before or after the space?

As a substantial donor to charities (**5**) .... recently gave £100m to Scottish schools, Mr Bennett's face often features in the newspapers. What is the secret to his success? Not the education system, (**6**) .... he says taught him little about business. It was his father (**7**) .... inspired him and it was his father's grocery business (**8**) .... Bennett borrowed that first £5,000 from.

> Is this referring to charities or to Mr Bennett?

> Did he borrow from a person?

Check your answers on page 88.

Prepositions with nouns and adjectives

It is important to learn common combinations of verbs, nouns and adjectives with prepositions because they often appear in this part of the test.

Complete the sentences below with a noun, verb or adjective from the box. Look at the preposition in each sentence to help you.

Nouns	Verbs
effect .....*on*.....	benefit ....
participation	depend ....
increase	cooperate ....
Adjectives	
acceptable	
familiar	
capable	

1   The recent interest rate rise has had a considerable negative ......*effect*...... on sales of our products.

2   We did not sign the contract as the terms were not .... to us.

3   Workers will .... from the proposed wage rise.

4   The old production line was not .... of meeting any rise in demand.

> This preposition is followed by the -ing form of a verb.

5   In order to meet the .... in demand, we recruited 50 more temporary staff.

6   Thanks to a successful advertising campaign, people all over the world are .... with our products.

7   To save money the two companies have decided to .... with each other in a new joint venture.

8   Next year's investment plans .... on many factors, including the political situation.

9   Union members are demanding more .... in planning the company strategy.

Now add the prepositions to the boxes to help you remember the combinations.

Check your answers on page 88.

Common mistakes

It is important to know what you should put in each space. It is also important to know what you should not put in each space.

The sentences below all contain common mistakes that people make in this section. The mistake in each sentence is <u>underlined</u>. Can you correct it?

1 It is customer care <u>what</u> *that* really matters in this company.

2 If very <u>little</u> people are interested in buying the product, you should relaunch it.

3 Sales were much higher <u>that</u> they had predicted.

4 A healthy working environment is the <u>more</u> important thing to consider.

5 There has been a rapid <u>decreasing</u> in the number of clients recently.

6 Cornet Ltd has chosen to <u>specialising</u> in IT consultancy.

7 We have decided to close the factory <u>that</u> we have been producing toys for 50 years.

8 This company wastes far too <u>many</u> energy by leaving computers on over the weekend.

Check your answers on page 88.

Linking words

Sometimes in this part of the test, you will find sentences where ideas are linked together with a missing linking word.

Complete the sentences with *so, and, or, because, also* or *although*.

1 I am writing to complain ..... *because* ..... the goods I ordered have not arrived.

2 The company is going to expand into both India .... China.

3 .... it will be a huge investment, we really must have that new machine.

4 We closed the old factory because it was becoming unprofitable. .... there were health and safety problems.

5 We can't afford to spend more money on either IT .... language training next year.

6 Demand has rocketed .... we need to recruit 200 new workers.

Check your answers on page 88.

Test practice

Now try this exercise. It is like the one you will see in the test. Read the text below and think of the word which best fits each space 1–5. Write only one word in each space.

Mission Statements

A good mission statement describes in a (**1**) .... words what your business is all about. It will be in plain language and will sound true to your staff and customers. Mission statements (**2**) .... claim the unbelievable – mission impossible – do more harm than good.

Mission statements are as old as modern business. In 1915 Citibank promised to become 'the most powerful'. (**3**) .... then, Disney have said they would 'make people happy' and Honda planned 'to destroy Yamaha'. Ironically, you may not need a mission statement at (**4**) .... If your company has real reason to exist, a visitor from another planet should be (**5**) .... of recognising your mission without reading it on paper first.

This is a plural, countable noun, so what should you use: 'few' or 'little'?

What word gives more information about things?

What word means from a time in the past until now?

This is part of an expression which means 'in any way'.

Do you remember this collocation from page 49?

Check your answers on page 89.

Now do the test on page 51.

Reading and Language Knowledge Test

Part Two
Section Three
Questions 87–91

- For questions **87–91**, read the text below and think of the word which best fits each space.
- Write only **one** word for each space on your Answer Sheet.

Example:

He is very interested (**0**) .... computers.

Answer:

0	in	▭ ▭

Wholesale Pallets

Wholesale pallets contain similar goods that have been batched together to be sold on at trade prices. For example, a wholesaler may offer an electronics pallet (**87**) .... may contain several TVs, DVD players and games consoles.

Pallets are a good example of why you should check the condition of wholesale goods before you buy them. They can be excellent buys (**88**) .... your business, and you can save a substantial amount of your wholesaling budget.

However, the downside is that they can be carelessly put together and the quality of the goods varies (**89**) .... batch to batch. Many pallets are unchecked by the wholesaler, (**90**) .... be particularly careful when buying them, as you may end up spending a lot of money on damaged goods. Get assurance from the wholesaler and if you are still not happy, the wholesaler should (**91**) .... you check the batches yourself.

Check your answers on page 89.

Reading and Language Knowledge Part 2, Section 4
Sentences with a gap (6 QUESTIONS)

This unit will help you to prepare for Part 2, Section 4 of the Reading and Language Knowledge Test. This part of BULATS tests your knowledge of grammar and vocabulary. In this part of the test, there are 6 questions. For each question you have to complete a sentence with the correct word. There are 4 options (A, B, C or D) for each question. You also saw this type of question in Part 1, Section 2, but in Part 2 the questions are generally more difficult.

Look back again at the information on page 31 for other ideas on how to prepare for this section. Look again at the practice exercises for that section as they will help you with Part 1, Section 2 and Part 2, Section 4.

Look at page 31 for an example question from this section of the test.

Practice exercises

Related words

Look at the words in the box below. Put the words in groups of similar meaning.

account administer ~~agenda~~ ~~boost~~
colleagues ~~deadly~~ grow hazardous
inspect invoice lethal list monitor
programme raise receipt refurbish
verify renovate restructure run
subordinates supervise workforce

increase *boost*

plan *agenda*

dangerous *deadly*

manage

improve

employees

bill

check

> Can you remember the ideas in Part 1, Section 2 for recording vocabulary? Have you used any of them?

Check your answers on page 89.

Now use a word from each group to complete the sentences.

1 As part of our modernisation scheme, we plan to totally .... the company at management level.

2 Please find enclosed our .... for the repair work carried out on 5th June.

3 If we employed someone to .... the goods before they left the factory, there would be fewer complaints.

4 Our graduate training .... is a vital part of our success.

5 Next year, staff can expect their salaries to .... by over 10%.

6 Health and safety rules require a member of staff to .... the unloading of all deliveries to the warehouse.

7 Notice: All .... waste should be disposed of in the special bins provided.

8 When the new plant opens, the .... will almost double.

Check your answers on page 89.

Completing gaps in sentences

It is sometimes a good idea to look at the sentence first without looking at the four options (A–D) as they can sometimes distract you from the correct answer.

Think of a word which could complete each sentence.

1 In this job, I can do things the way I like and I really enjoy that ....

2 Moving the company makes good sense .... We'd be closer to our customers.

3 I expect this company to develop into a major .... in the IT industry.

4 One of our suppliers was .... bankrupt last month.

5 If we don't complete the work on time, there's a .... clause of $4,000 per day.

6 We increased production to meet the recent .... in demand.

How many answers are you sure about? Now look at the next exercise.

Choosing the correct definition

In this exercise, we are going to think more about what the missing words might mean.

With each sentence there are 2 definitions of the missing word. Which sounds most suitable?

1 In this job, I can do things the way I like and I really enjoy that .... *a* ....

  a a noun which means freedom and the power to make your own decisions

  b a noun which means being controlled by others; a lack of freedom

You probably would not enjoy a lack of freedom.

2 Moving the company makes good sense .... We'd be closer to our customers.

  a an adverb connected with organising and planning something

  b an adverb connected with equality and behaving in an appropriate way

3 I expect this company to develop into a major .... in the IT industry.

  a a noun which means performing a role or pretending to be someone else

  b a noun which means taking part in competition with others

4 One of our suppliers was .... bankrupt last month.

  a a verb which means to announce something

  b a verb which means to use strength or power to make someone do something they don't want to do

5 If we don't complete the work on time, there's a .... clause of $4,000 per day.

  a a noun which means a benefit or profit

  b a noun which means a punishment for doing something wrong

6 We increased production to meet the recent .... in demand.

  a a noun which means something of a higher standard or quality

  b a noun which means an upward movement

Check your answers on page 89.

Test practice

Now try this exercise. It is similar to the one you will see in the test.

Choose the word or phrase which best completes each sentence. Remember your answers to the last exercise. Use them to help you choose the correct option (A–D) in this exercise.

1 In this job, I can do things the way I like and I really enjoy that ....

  A dependence

  B autonomy

  C permission

  D reliance

Which of these words has a similar meaning to the definition from the previous exercise?

2 Moving the company makes good sense .... We'd be much closer to our customers.

  A conveniently

  B suitably

  C reasonably

  D logistically

One of these is connected with organising something. Which one?

3 I expect this company to develop into a major .... in the IT industry.

  A actor

  B member

  C player

  D component

Many games involve competition. Which of these words could be connected to games?

4 One of our suppliers was .... bankrupt last month.

  A declared

  B forced

  C turned

  D stated

Which of these means to announce something?

5 If we don't complete the work on time, there's a .... clause of $4,000 per day.

  A reward

  B consequence

  C penalty

  D fine

Two words here mean a punishment, but only one is used in business. Which one?

6 We increased production to meet the recent .... in demand.

  A upside

  B upgrade

  C uplift

  D upturn

Only one of these words describes an upwards movement. Which one?

Check your answers on page 89.

Now do the test on pages 54–55.

Reading and Language Knowledge Test

Part Two
Section Four
Questions 92–97

- Choose the word or phrase which best completes each sentence.
- For questions **92–97**, mark **one** letter **A**, **B**, **C** or **D** on your Answer Sheet.

92 Here is the list of the .... of the direct marketing leaflets.

    A receptions

    B receivers

    C recipients

    D receipts

93 We need to drive down costs to .... profit margins.

    A further

    B heighten

    C boost

    D advance

94 Have you decided how much time to .... to each interview?

    A distribute

    B allocate

    C divide

    D share

95 More and more companies are using the internet for the .... of recruitment.

   A rationale

   B function

   C purpose

   D use

96 Having their own transport is an essential .... when we select a suitable postholder.

   A principle

   B criterion

   C measurement

   D standard

97 Very few deals go through .... from beginning to end.

   A smoothly

   B evenly

   C flatly

   D consistently

Check your answers on page 89.

Reading and Language Knowledge Part 2, Section 5
Understanding a longer text (6 QUESTIONS)

This unit will help you to prepare for Part 2, Section 5 of the Reading and Language Knowledge Test. This part of BULATS tests your knowledge of longer pieces of writing. You read a text and answer 6 multiple-choice questions. You also saw this type of question in Part 1, Section 3, but in Part 2 there are 4 options (A, B, C or D) for each question.

Read the advice on page 34 again. It will also help you to prepare for this part of the test.

> **More points to remember**
> - Read all the text first to help you understand the topic.
> - Don't worry if you do not understand some words. It will still be possible to answer the questions.
> - Before you answer any questions, read all of them.
> - As you answer each question, mark the place in the text where you found the answer. This will help you to check your answers at the end.
> - Answer the questions you are most confident about first – don't spend too long on a question. If you still don't know the answer at the end, remember to guess.

Here is an example of a question from Part 2, Section 5 of the Reading and Language Knowledge Test:

> **Part Two**
> **Section Five**
> **Questions 98–103**
>
> - Read the article below about data mining and answer questions **98–103** on the opposite page.
> - For questions **98–103**, mark **one** letter **A, B, C** or **D** on your Answer Sheet.

Read these instructions carefully. They tell you what you're reading (e.g. an article), and what it is about (e.g. data mining).

Practice exercise

In this section, you are going to practise looking for information in a text. The text in this exercise is about data mining (how companies can use old data to improve their services).

In the test, the text comes before the questions, but it can be useful to read the questions first.

Look at questions 1–4 below, but cover up the possible answers A–D. Then read the text and think about the answers to questions 1–4 without looking at answers A–D.

1 In the first paragraph, the writer says old data is like oil because
  A finding it is an expensive process.
  B it is hard to process.
  C it has to be looked for.
  D it is very valuable for the finder.

If you are sure an answer is wrong, cross it out.

2 To get useful information from data mining you need
  A trained staff.
  B a lot of time.
  C the right technology.
  D to know customer details.

Remember: if you don't know the answer, guess! You have a 1 in 4 chance of being correct. You do not lose marks if your answer is wrong.

3 In the third paragraph, what does the writer think is the most useful product of data mining?
  A obtaining the customers' home addresses
  B creating customer profiles
  C learning details of the different companies a customer uses
  D knowing the most popular products on the market

4 According to the writer, why should older companies use data mining?
  A They are losing market share to younger companies.
  B They need to update their databases.
  C Their knowledge of their customers could be an advantage.
  D They need to save money on customer care.

Now look at the options A, B, C and D for each question 1–4. Are your answers the same as any of the options? Look at the text again and choose the best option.

> *Underline the place in the text where you think the answer is. You can check this in the key later.*

DATA MINING

Put simply, data mining is like drilling for oil. Instead of expensive rigs, computer software searches for lost data that has lain forgotten in archives and files, sometimes for years. Frequently, companies are
5 not even aware that they have this data as filing systems change and cost-conscious new managers fail to upgrade old databases. Like oil, old data is there, waiting to be discovered.

Data mining can produce vast quantities of
10 information. The key is knowing what you are looking for. With the latest software it needn't take forever provided you ask the right questions. Without proper analysis, however, this data is of no value whatsoever. The real value of the data lies not
15 in the millions of facts and figures it may contain, but in analysing it to reveal previously undiscovered customer information.

Just imagine this scenario: a customer uses a credit card to buy goods. The same customer then buys
20 some gifts from a catalogue, then buys a new car … and so it continues. A series of transactions, all from the same address, but through different companies and on different databases. With intelligent data mining, incredibly detailed files on customers can be
25 created, stored and used as the basis of the next marketing campaign.

Nowhere is data mining more necessary than in old, established industries such as telecoms and insurance, which have dominated their markets for
30 years. Yet now this dominance may be at risk from newer companies with better organised systems. These older companies have one weapon left: they may have enormous databases twenty or more years old and all the information in them could be just
35 what they need to stay on top.

Before you check your answers, do the next exercises.

A closer look at the text

1 Answer the following questions.

a What words in paragraph 1 mean *looks for something*?

....

b What noun in paragraph 2 is connected with technology?

....

c What kind of information could be found in *files on customers* (line 24)?

....

d What does the expression *just what they need* (lines 34–35) mean?

....

2 There are some useful words and expressions in this text. Match the words and expressions a–h to the definitions 1–8.

a rigs (line 2)

b has lain forgotten (line 3)

c not even aware that (line 5)

d cost-conscious (line 6)

e the key is (line 10)

f it needn't take forever (lines 11–12)

g is of no value whatsoever (lines 13–14)

h weapon (line 32)

1 the most important thing

2 to have no use or importance at all

3 to be perhaps quicker than you think

4 equipment used to drill for oil

5 knowledge or information used to fight against something/somebody

6 has been inactive or unused for a long period of time

7 to not know about or realise something

8 to be worried about saving money

Check your answers for the exercises above on page 90, then look back at the reading exercise on page 56. Do you want to change any of your answers before you check them? Then check your answers on page 90.

Now do the test on pages 58–59.

Reading and Language Knowledge Test

Part Two
Section Five
Questions 98–103

- Read the article below about outsourcing, and answer questions **98–103** on the opposite page.
- For questions **98–103**, mark **one** letter **A**, **B**, **C** or **D** on your Answer Sheet.

Outsource in haste

In recent years, many top European companies have decided to go down the outsourcing route. Last year, the fastest growth in the outsourcing of business processes occurred in the types of companies who can outsource services for contracts worth in excess of €50 million. Financial services (38%) and manufacturing (17%) are the business functions most commonly involved in such arrangements, but human resources showed the greatest growth of all outsourced functions.

When a company wants to focus on its core business, cut costs or exploit the expertise of specialists, outsourcing certain of its functions may be the best answer. In many cases it makes strategic sense. The vendor (i.e. the provider of the outsourced service) is able to focus on the outsourced function as a core competence, and can bring greater economies of scale and deeper knowledge and expertise in specific areas. Many firms agree to outsourcing in the belief that it will allow them to concentrate on strategic growth, reduce headcount and redirect capital budget.

However, decisions on outsourcing should be made extremely cautiously, or the vendor will be the only one reaping real benefits, while the purchasing company (i.e. the company which outsources services and buys them in) ends up giving money away. A firm that fails to calculate its in-house costs properly will make false comparisons with the cost of outsourcing. One manufacturing business, for example, had a small internal audit department with a staff of nine which had been costing them €500,000 a year to run. They outsourced and paid €350,000 per year to the vendor. However, at the vendor's rate, this paid for just three people, who did the job adequately. The company had just thought that it was ridding itself of a problem and saving money but in fact was paying over the odds for three people who it could have hired more cheaply in-house.

The trap into which firms are falling is failing to sort out department problems before outsourcing – and of course it is the 'problem' departments that are most usually outsourced. Before taking the plunge, a company should investigate any existing problems in the function they are considering outsourcing, solve them, and only then decide if outsourcing is the best option.

Outsourcing is a complex endeavour. Without clear direction, the process can become prolonged, expensive and frustrating. Outsourcing is generally a long-term contractual relationship, and over the contract term, the customer's business, competitive and regulatory environments may change dramatically. Before outsourcing, the company must decide what it wants to achieve within a specific time-frame, and make those expectations clear in the agreement with the vendor.

Firms should approach outsourcing by first defining their business processes and understanding all the inputs and outputs in detail. Then, having reviewed where improvements might be made and inefficiencies eliminated, they are in a stronger position to negotiate with any vendor. The firm can then provide a list of each of their business tasks in detail and show whether the firm or a potential vendor is responsible for carrying out the tasks. However, in many cases, the review process is so beneficial that the function that was to be outsourced is, in the end, kept in-house. After all, if you outsource, someone else is making the money instead of you. Think carefully before relinquishing the chance to make a profit.

98 What kind of businesses have most increased their outsourcing arrangements recently?

   A   companies in the financial services industry

   B   companies involved in deals above a certain value

   C   manufacturing companies

   D   companies which operate outside Europe

99 What does 'headcount' mean in the second paragraph?

   A   different kinds of companies

   B   number of experts

   C   varieties of business functions

   D   staffing levels

100 What was the mistake that the manufacturing business made?

   A   They paid more to the vendor than they had paid to run their in-house operation.

   B   They failed to save any money through outsourcing.

   C   They miscalculated how much they needed to pay to run the function themselves.

   D   They used a company who had insufficient skilled staff.

101 The writer says that 'problem departments' should be

   A   used in experiments to assess the suitability of outsourcing.

   B   sorted out before being considered for outsourcing.

   C   kept out of any plans for outsourcing.

   D   chosen before other departments for outsourcing.

102 In the fifth paragraph, what advice does the writer give about outsourcing?

   A   Set time constraints on the delivery of results from the outsourcing relationship.

   B   Research what is likely to happen during the life of the outsourcing agreement.

   C   Write conditions into the contract covering you against any unexpected events.

   D   Avoid agreeing terms which will tie you to one vendor for a long period.

103 What is the writer's main point about the use of outsourcing in the text as a whole?

   A   Outsourcing can only benefit certain business processes.

   B   Outsourcing may lose firms opportunities to gain profits for themselves.

   C   Outsourcing will start to lose its popularity in the near future.

   D   Outsourcing relationships are more trouble than they're worth.

Check your answers on page 90.

Reading and Language Knowledge Part 2, Section 6

Correcting errors in a text (7 QUESTIONS)

This unit will help you to prepare for Part 2, Section 6 of the Reading and Language Knowledge Test. This part of BULATS tests grammar and vocabulary. In this section, you read a text of 100–150 words. There are 7 lines which are tested. Some lines have a mistake in them. You have to decide which lines have a mistake and then correct the mistake. There could be 1, 2 or 3 correct lines.

The things most commonly tested are:

- tenses
- verb forms
- *-ing* or *to*
- modal verbs
- *which, that, who, whose, where, what*
- countable and uncountable nouns
- conditional sentences
- comparatives
- passives
- cause and effect phrases

Here is an example of a question from Part 2, Section 6 of the Reading and Language Knowledge Test:

Part Two
Section Six
Questions 104–110

This tells you who wrote the text and why.

- A colleague has written this letter to a customer and has asked you to check it.
- In some lines there is one wrong word.

Remember that some lines are correct!

- If there is a wrong word, write the correct word on your Answer Sheet.
- If there is no mistake, put a tick (✓) on your Answer Sheet.

Example:
0   One of the items you ordered from our
00 catalogue is <u>temporary</u> out of stock.

0	✓
00	*temporarily*

Remember to complete the Answer Sheet clearly.

Practice exercises

The exercises below practise correcting some of the most common types of mistake you will see in Section 6.

Verb forms

Find the mistake in each sentence, then cross it out and correct it.

1 The location of the meeting has been ~~choosing~~. *chosen*

2 Working at full capacity we are made 500 units a day at the moment.

3 Our new shop has open for business next month.

4 When we launched our new product, our competitor had already launching theirs.

5 My company was just bought a new phone system.

6 The parent company was establish in 1778.

7 Call 0123 536 782 if you needed any more details.

8 I will let you know when we planned our next meeting.

Check your answers on page 90.

Mistakes with plurals

Section 6 often includes a mistake with plurals. It might be the use of a singular noun instead of a plural, or an uncountable noun instead of a countable noun.

How many of these sentences with plurals are correct?

1 There are a number of possible time we could meet.

2 This consultancy offers advices in financial matters.

3 This is one of the most important piece of information in your contract.

4 There has been a great deal of investment in this project, but only a little progress.

5 The training budget can be reduced as enough worker have now been trained.

6 We have not had any monthly payments for the technical equipment we supplied you with.

7 The sales figure have improved month on month since we started discounting.

8 Our revolutionary new product is the result of extensive researches.

Check your answers on page 90.

Mistakes with *which, that, who, whose, where* and *what*

You have seen some examples of this area of grammar before (see page 49). This section looks at typical mistakes made with these words.

Complete the sentences with *which, that, who, whose, where* and *what* to remind yourself how to use the words correctly.

> *This is emphasising the single best thing about the company.*

1 .... I like best about this company is the way they look after their staff.

2 I don't know .... designed this product, but they are in the wrong job!

> *Is this describing a person or a thing?*

3 Our database helps us select the jobs .... are right for you, ... guarantees we never waste your time.

> *'Which' or 'that' after a comma?*

4 IT is an area .... we can make real progress in the future.

5 The management has agreed .... Health and Safety training will be a priority.

> *This word is introducing a new part of the sentence.*

6 Alan Dickinson, ... appointment to the Board was only made last month, has decided to step down due to family reasons.

> *Which word can be used to describe something relating to or belonging to a person?*

Check your answers on page 90. Then see if you can correct these sentences.

7 Please return the invoice what we sent you, as it contains an error.

8 Lausanne Holdings AG have announced which they will be opening an office in Paris next year.

9 The conference was held in London, that was a very popular choice.

10 I'm afraid I can't help. You'll have to speak to the person whose is responsible.

11 Prices have fallen to the point that production is no longer economic.

12 The new CEO, which had only been in the job for six months, was fired suddenly yesterday.

Check your answers on pages 90–91.

Test practice

Now try this exercise. It is like the one you will see in the test.

A colleague has written this letter to a new customer and has asked you to check it. There is one correct line. Read the letter. Can you identify the correct line? Check your answer on page 91.

Now correct the other mistakes. Here are some suggestions to help you find them:
- **One line has a mistake with a passive.**
- **One line has a mistake with a tense.**
- **One line has a mistake with reporting what someone said.**
- **One line has a mistake with a pronoun.**
- **One line has a mistake with a plural.**

> *Always remember to look at the lines before and after the line you are studying.*

Dear Mr Cooper
1 ......on...... I very much enjoyed meeting you at Tuesday. Thank you for giving
2 .... me the opportunities to present our new product line and for agreeing
3 .... to stock it in your chain of shops. Can I just confirm some of the
4 .... details of our agreement? You agreed to my company will supply
5 .... our full range of products to all 18 of yours shops and, in addition, we
6 .... have stock an agreed range of spare parts. Payment will be by bank
7 .... transfer after 60 days. We will deliver 48 hours after an order has being
placed with us.
If possible we would like to sign the contract by 23rd of this month.
Yours sincerely
Robin Gray
Sales Manager

Check your answers on page 91.

Now do the test on page 62.

Reading and Language Knowledge Test

Part Two
Section Six
Questions 104–110

- A colleague of yours has written a letter and asked you to check it.
- In some lines there is one wrong word.
- If there is a wrong word, write the correct word on your Answer Sheet.
- If there is no mistake, put a tick (✓) on your Answer Sheet.

Example:

One of the items you ordered from our

catalogue is <u>temporary</u> out of stock.

0	✓
00	*temporarily*

	Dear Maria
104	I am writing to tell you that the day for the IT training has been deciding.
105	It has take place on Thursday 3rd March in the IT Department at the West Site from 9.30
106	to 4.30. I realise that this is one of the date when you were unavailable, but unfortunately,
107	it was the most convenient date for the majority of the staff who expressed an interest. If
108	you can subsequently able to attend the training on this day, please let me know and I will
109	add you at the list of attendees. Otherwise, I will inform you when we next organise an IT
110	training day. Please do not hesitate to contact me if you required any further information.
	Yours sincerely
	Graham Harris
	Harris IT Services

Check your answers on page 91.

The BULATS Writing Test

The BULATS Writing Test takes 45 minutes. The test is divided into 2 parts.

Here are some more details about the 2 parts:

	Part 1	**Part 2**
You will read	• information such as a short letter, an email or an advertisement	• background information on a situation and instructions telling you what to write
You will write	• a short message or letter	• a report or letter
Number of words	• 50–60 words	• 180–200 words
Time	• about 15 minutes	• about 30 minutes
Number of questions	• 1 question which you must answer	• choose 1 question from 2 options (A or B)

Examiners are looking for the following things when they mark your Writing Test:

Assessment in the BULATS Writing Test
- If you can use correct vocabulary and grammar without making too many mistakes.
- If you can use different types of grammar, from basic structures up to more advanced ones, and how much vocabulary you know.
- If your style of writing is appropriate. In BULATS you should use a neutral or formal style because this is more suitable for most business writing.
- If you can organise your answer well. This means 2 things:
  - the way you organise your answer as a whole (e.g. using appropriate paragraphs for the introduction, the middle section and the conclusion).
  - the way you organise your ideas in each paragraph. (If your ideas are easy to follow and linked effectively, you will usually get a better grade.)
- If you answer the question. In each question there are 3 points you must write about. Always check that you have done this before you finish. If you miss any of these points, you will lose marks.

Points to remember
- Your answers to Part 1 and Part 2 are assessed separately. If you have problems with Part 1, for example, it will not affect your grade for Part 2.
- You should try not to copy words or expressions from the question. This will not help your grade. It is always best to use your own words.
- Good spelling is important. Always take time to check your spelling after you finish writing your answer. If you make too many spelling mistakes, you will lose marks.
- Plan your answer before you write, e.g. you have about 30 minutes for Part 2 so you can plan for 5 minutes and write for 25 minutes.

Writing Part 1
Short message/letter (50–60 words)

This unit will help you to prepare for Part 1 of the Writing Test. In this part of the test, you write a short message (memo or email) or letter.

Here is an example of a question from Part 1 of the Writing Test:

Part One

You work in the Human Resources department of a large company. You have received this email.

> To: HR department
> From: Amanda Pearson
> Subject: Job interview
>
> Dear Sir/Madam
> I should be attending an interview at your company for the job of office assistant on Friday at 15.00, but have been ill this week. I am writing to ask if it is possible to re-arrange the interview for a later date. I am available for interview any day next week.
> Best regards
> Amanda Pearson

Write an **email** to Ms Pearson.
- thank her for her email;
- give details of a new interview date;
- ask her to bring a copy of her CV.
Write about **50–60 words** on the opposite page.

Test practice (1)

Complete the spaces in this sample answer with a suitable expression.

Use the name if there is one in the question.

Does this answer include all three points in the question?

Dear Ms Pearson

(**1**) _Thank you for your email_ regarding re-arranging your interview. I am sorry to hear you have been ill.
(**2**) .... arrange another time for your interview. (**3**) ....
come at 3.00 on Monday 15th May?
(**4**) .... you could bring a copy of your CV with you to the interview.

Best regards
Michael Kennedy

You don't need to include 'Dear …' and 'Best regards' in your word count.

Don't check your answers at this stage.

Writing practice

This exercise gives examples of typical language you will need for Part 1 of the Writing Test.

Match phrases a–h with functions 1–4 and phrases i–n with functions 5–7. There are 2 answers for each function.

1 apologise .... c ....

In every Part 1 writing question you will have to use this type of language. Can you think of any more examples of this type of language?

2 thank ....

3 request/ask ....

4 suggest ....

a Would you be able to …?
b I am grateful for …
c I am sorry for …
d I would like to recommend …
e I would be grateful if you could …
f I am afraid I will not be able to …
g We should …
h Thank you for your email regarding …

5 offer ....

This language can also be useful for letters in Part 2.

6 explain ....

7 invite ....

i This is because …
j Would you be available next week?
k Due to the fact that …
l Would you like me to …?
m I would like to invite you to …
n I would be happy to …

Check your answers on page 91. There are more examples of this kind of language on page 27.

Test practice (2)

Look at Test practice (1) again. Do you want to change any of your answers using language from the Writing practice exercise above? When you have finished, check your answers on page 91.

Now do the test on page 65.

Writing Test

Part One

You are making a speech at a conference and have received this fax from the conference organiser.

Fax

From: **John Mason**

Subject: Arrangements for Conference

Thank you for agreeing to speak at our conference. I have arranged for a taxi to collect you from your hotel at 8 am. Please could you confirm that this time is convenient and let me know what equipment you need for your talk.

Write a **fax** in reply:

- confirm the taxi time;
- give details of any equipment needed;
- ask for a conference programme.

Write about **50–60 words**.

Write your answers to Part One here. Do not write addresses as part of your answer.

Fax

To: **John Mason**

From:

Subject: Arrangements for Conference

_____

_____

_____

_____

_____

_____

_____

_____

_____

Look at the sample answer on page 91.

Writing Part 2
Report or letter (180–200 words)

This unit will help you to prepare for Part 2 of the Writing Test. In this part of the test, you write a report or a letter.

Here is an example of a question from Part 2 of the Writing Test:

> **Part Two**
>
> The company you work for is deciding whether to buy a bigger office building. The Managing Director has asked you to write a report with your recommendations about this.
>
> Write the **report** for the Managing Director, making your recommendations.
>
> Write about:
> - why a bigger office building might be needed;
> - where the best location would be for the new offices;
> - what facilities the new offices should have
>
> and any other points which you think are important.
>
> Write about **180–200 words** on the following pages.

Writing practice

Answer these questions about the test question above.

1 Who will read this report? *(Ask yourself the same questions for a letter.)*

2 How many points have to be included in your answer?

3 Will the report include a conclusion?

4 What is the maximum and minimum length of the report?

These are all very important questions to ask yourself when you prepare to write your answer.

Check your answers on page 91.

Test practice

Use these phrases to complete the sample answer.

it is concluded that	it was found that
this would mean that	it is recommended that
~~the aim of this report is to~~	due to the fact that
in addition	

Report on New Offices

Giving clear headings can help with good organisation. Before you start writing, make a plan.

Introduction

(**1**) *The aim of this report is to* examine the advantages of moving to a bigger office building than our current location.

Why new premises?

(**2**) .... this company is expanding rapidly, we will need to recruit another fifty administrative and sales staff within the next three months. After studying the office facilities, (**3**) .... there is no more space available for additional staff and we therefore need to find bigger offices urgently.

This shows the examiner you have included all three content points.

Location

The best location for a new office building would be on the east side of the town with good access to the roads and trains. (**4**) .... our staff and visitors would be able to get to the offices quicker.

Facilities needed

The offices should be at least 50% bigger than our present offices. They should be fully air conditioned and they must have fast internet access. (**5**) .... , there should be good car parking space for our staff and visitors.

Conclusion

(**6**) .... the current offices are no longer suitable and (**7**) .... we begin looking for new offices that meet our needs as soon as possible.

Check your answers on page 91.

Now do the test on page 67.

Writing Test

Part Two

EITHER

Task A

Your department is spending a lot of money on its travel and entertainment expenses. You have been asked by the Finance Director to write a report about this.

Write a **report** to the Finance Director.

Write about:

- what travel and entertainment you are spending the money on;
- why this spending is necessary;
- how this spending could be reduced

and any other points which you think are important.

Write about **180–200 words**.

OR

Task B

Your Group Manager has asked you to write a report about office space in your department.

Write a **report** to the Group Manager.

Write about:

- the problems of space in your department;
- the effects of this on your department;
- your recommendations for improving the situation

and any other points which you think are important.

Write about **180–200 words**.

Look at the sample answers on page 92.

The BULATS Speaking Test

The BULATS Speaking Test takes about 12 minutes. There are 2 people involved: the BULATS examiner and you. The test is recorded so there will be a microphone on the table. Do not worry! This is just to help with the assessment.

The Speaking Test is divided into 3 parts. Here is some information about them:

	The examiner	You
Speaking Part 1 (about 4 minutes)	• asks you questions about yourself including your job or studies and your personal interests	• answer the examiner's questions and talk about these topics
Speaking Part 2 (about 4 minutes)	• gives you a piece of paper with 3 presentation topics on it • listens to your presentation • asks 1 or 2 questions after your presentation	• choose 1 topic • spend 1 minute preparing the topic • talk about the topic for 1 minute • answer 1 or 2 questions from the examiner connected to the topic
Speaking Part 3 (about 4 minutes)	• gives you a piece of paper with a role-play situation explained on it • takes part in the role-play • discusses a topic connected to the role-play with you	• spend 1 minute reading and thinking about the situation • ask the examiner questions in the role-play to find out missing information • discuss a topic connected to the role-play with the examiner

When you take the Speaking Test, the examiner will assess your speaking. You will also be recorded. The recording is sent to another examiner who will listen to your test and assess your speaking in more detail. The examiners are listening for the following things:

Assessment in the BULATS Speaking Test
- If you are fluent, which means how well you can speak with only natural hesitations, and if you can organise what you want to say.
- If you can use correct vocabulary and grammar without making too many mistakes.
- If you can use different types of grammar, from basic structures up to more advanced ones, and how much vocabulary you know.
- If your pronunciation is clear and understandable.
- If you need help from the examiner during the test and if you can have a natural conversation with the examiner.

Preparation tips

- Think about how good you are at the things which are assessed in the Speaking Test. Ask a teacher, or an English-speaking friend or colleague, to give you some comments or suggestions on your English.
- If you can, record yourself and listen. What do you think you could do better?
- For Speaking Part 1, if you have a teacher, or an English-speaking friend or colleague, try answering questions on the topics on page 70 with them. Try to speak naturally, not like an actor.
- For Speaking Part 2, practise reading aloud for 1 minute (use an English book) so you know how much time you will have to speak for.
- For Speaking Part 3, study how to make questions as you will have to ask the examiner questions to find out information.
- Remember, all speaking practice is useful.

Speaking Part 1 Interview

This unit will help you to prepare for Part 1 of the Speaking Test. This part of the test takes about 4 minutes. In this part of the test, the examiner will ask you some questions about yourself. The questions will include some of the topics in the table below.

Everyone has to answer questions from this topic.

Topic	You will talk about
1 Introduction	yourself, where you live and where you study or work
2 Current work	your job, if you have one
3 Current studies	your studies, if you are a student
4 Travel	places you have been
5 Language learning	your experiences of learning English and your opinions on language learning
6 Future career prospects or plans	what you might do in the future in your working life
7 Personal interests	what you like to do in your free time

Everyone has to answer questions from one of the topics 4–7.

Test preparation

Here are some ways you can prepare for the questions the examiner might ask you in Part 1:

1 Look at each of the topics and think about some of the things you might talk to the examiner about.

Some people find it useful to make lists of information like this:

> **My studies**
>
> Details: I study …
>
>   My studies involve …
>
> Good points: The most interesting thing about my studies is …
>
> Bad points: One thing I don't like is …

2 Think about questions the examiner might ask. How can you answer these questions? For example, if you are a student at the moment, what questions could you ask other students about their studies?

3 Remember to ask the examiner if there is anything you don't understand.

4 If you know someone who speaks English, or who is also going to take the BULATS Speaking Test, practise with them. Prepare questions together and practise asking and answering them together.

5 Remember, this part is only 4 minutes long. You don't have to give very long answers for each question.

But yes or no answers are usually not enough!

Useful language

Look at the different things you might be asked about in the Speaking Test. Match the sentences a–g with the topics 1–7.

1 Introduction …e..

2 Current work ……

3 Current studies ……

4 Travel ……

5 Language learning ……

6 Future career prospects or plans ……

7 Personal interests ……

What do you think the questions were here?

a I'm in the Sales department. I've been there for a year.

b I'd like to work in Marketing, if I get the chance.

c I like talking to people from different countries.

d I've always liked skiing. I go every weekend in the winter.

e My surname is Knudsen. That's K-N-U-D-S-E-N.

f The best place I've ever been is Rome.

g I'm doing a degree in Computer Science.

Make sure you can spell your name if the examiner asks.

Check your answers on page 92.

Now do the test on page 71.

Speaking Test

Part One: Interview (about 4 minutes)

The examiner asks you questions about yourself, your work and your interests.

Speaking Part 2 Presentation

This unit will help you to prepare for Part 2 of the Speaking Test. In this part of the test, you have to speak for 1 minute on a topic which the examiner will give to you. These topics are always related to real situations. Usually you need to:

- talk about something your company does, has done, or plans to do, or

Remember: this will affect the tenses you use.

- talk about something you do, have done, or plan to do.

Here is an example of part of a question from Part 2 of the Speaking Test:

Part Two
INSTRUCTIONS

Please read all **THREE** topics below carefully.

Choose **ONE** which you feel you will be able to talk about for one minute.

Very important!

You have one minute to read and prepare your talk.

You may make notes.

Don't spend your time writing sentences. Use only key words.

Remember: you will have 3 choices in the actual test.

Topic A

Talk about a meeting you attended.

You should say:

You have to talk about these 3 things. Remember: you only have 1 minute.

- what the meeting was about;
- who was at the meeting;
- how you prepared for the meeting.

Was the meeting successful? Why? / Why not?

The examiner will ask you this question after your presentation.

Test practice (sample answers)

Look at the question above. Take 1 minute to make notes on what you would say about this topic. Time yourself.

If you can, record yourself and listen. What do you think you could do better?

🎧 22, 23 Now listen to the presentations given by two candidates. Do both candidates talk about all three points in the question?

Check your answers in the recording scripts on page 92.

Listen again. Which presentation is better, 1 or 2? Why?

When you have finished listening, look at the comments about each presentation on page 93.

Practice exercise

Look at the example question on the left. In this part of the test, you have to talk about the 3 points described in the question. If you like, you can add other details, but remember the examiner will stop you if you speak for much more than 1 minute and you must talk about the 3 points in the question.

Candidate 1 says: *I prepared for the meeting by ... , but I also ... .*

I also ... is used to give extra information.

Complete these sentences which contain useful language for adding extra information. The first letter of each missing word is given.

1 A nother .... important thing to remember is ...
2 In a.................... I think you should ...
3 I also b.................... that ...
4 Something e.................... you could do is ...
5 One m.................... thing is ...
6 I should have s.................... that ...

Use this when you have forgotten to include some information earlier.

7 As w.................... as ..., it's also a good idea to ...
8 Not o.................... do I ..., I also ...

Use these sentences to link 2 ideas.

Check your answers on page 93.

Now do the test on page 73.

Speaking Test

Part Two: Presentation (about 4 minutes)

The examiner gives you a sheet with three topics on it. You choose a topic and have one minute to prepare a short presentation. You speak on the topic for one minute. Afterwards, the examiner asks you one or two questions about your presentation.

TASK SHEET

> **INSTRUCTIONS**
>
> Please read all **THREE** topics below carefully.
> Choose **ONE** which you feel you will be able to talk about for one minute.
>
> You have one minute to read and prepare your talk.
> You may make notes.

Topic A

Describe the most recent product your company has manufactured.

You should say:
- what this product is;
- how easy it is to produce;
- how successful this product has been.

Would you like to change anything about this product? Why? / Why not?

Topic B

Describe how your company chooses its suppliers.

You should say:
- who chooses your company's suppliers;
- what your company expects from its suppliers;
- what happens if a supplier's service is unsatisfactory.

How satisfied is your company with its suppliers?

Topic C

Talk about how your company decided on the pricing of its products.

You should say:
- who decides on pricing;
- how decisions on pricing are made;
- how often prices are reviewed.

Could your company reduce its prices? Why? / Why not?

Speaking Part 3 — Information exchange and discussion

This unit will help you to prepare for Part 3 of the Speaking Test. In this part of the test, you take part in a role-play and a discussion with the examiner. This part of the test takes about 4 minutes.

The examiner will give you a piece of paper like the example below, with a role-play situation explained on it. In the role-play, you have to find out 3 items of information described in the question. After you have found out the information, you have to discuss a question related to the role-play situation with the examiner. This discussion is only 1 to 2 minutes long.

Here is an example of a question from Part 3 of the Speaking Test:

> **Part Three**
> **A New Job**
>
> You have one minute to read through this task.
>
> **Information Exchange**
> You are applying for the job of IT Manager at a local company.
> The examiner is the Human Resources Manager at the company. You are meeting him/her to find out more about the job.
>
> Find out this information: 1 job responsibilities
> 2 salary
> 3 other benefits offered
>
> You will then be asked to give your opinion on this information.
>
> **Discussion**
> Now discuss this topic with the examiner.
>
> > What is the best way to prepare for a job interview?

Use this time carefully. Read the question. Think about the questions you will need to ask.

Ask the examiner if you don't understand what to do.

You have to ask the examiner questions to find out this information.

Test preparation

Making questions to ask the examiner

Look again at the example question and the 3 pieces of information you have to find out. Think about what questions you need to ask the examiner.

Check your answers on page 93.

Preparing for the discussion

In this section of Part 3, you take part in a short discussion with the examiner about the topic at the bottom of the question paper. In the example question, this is:

> What is the best way to prepare for a job interview?

Remember: it doesn't matter if you don't know much about the topic. This is a test of English, not business knowledge.

You will need to give your opinion and reasons for this opinion. You might need to agree or disagree with something the examiner says.

Match the sentences a–h with the functions 1–4.

1 Giving an opinion ...*a*.... ....

2 Giving reasons ....

3 Agreeing ....

4 Disagreeing ....

a You should always be on time.

b I don't think that's true.

c That's because you need to create a good impression.

d That's right!

e I'm not sure that's a good idea.

f The most important thing to do is be positive.

g Yes, I think so.

h Wearing the right clothes means you will give a good impression in the interview.

Check your answers on page 93.

Now do the test on page 75.

Speaking Test

Part Three: Information Exchange and Discussion (about 4 minutes)

The examiner gives you a sheet with a role-play situation. You ask the examiner questions to get the required information. This leads to a discussion on a related topic.

TASK SHEET

> Factory Space

You have one minute to read through this task.

Information Exchange

You are looking for a factory for your company to rent. The examiner is the agent for an available factory. You want to find out whether the factory is suitable to rent.

Find out this information:

          1 factory location
          2 size of factory
          3 cost of renting

You will then be asked to give your opinion on this information.

Discussion

Now discuss this topic with the examiner.

> What do companies need to consider when choosing new premises?

The BULATS Computer Test

The BULATS Computer Test assesses your skills in reading, listening, grammar and vocabulary. It does not test your writing or speaking skills. Questions are presented on screen and you have to answer them using the mouse to click on the correct option or the computer keyboard to write your answers.

The length of the Computer Test varies for different candidates but will usually take about 1 hour. The test administrator might in some circumstances set a time limit of 75 minutes. When a time limit is set, the administrator will normally ensure a timer is displayed so that candidates know how much time they have left to complete the test.

There are 8 types of question in the Computer Test.

The skills tested in the Computer Test are similar to those tested in the Standard Test. The insert for each section tells you the corresponding Standard Test section. This will help you to prepare for the Computer Test.

Listening questions

Question type	You will hear	Your task
1 Listen and Select (text)	A short recording. This might be: • a monologue or dialogue • a telephone conversation or message • a public announcement • a face-to face conversation 🎧 *listen twice*	• a short multiple-choice question • 3 or 4 options to click on for each question (A, B, C or D) • all three options are written `Listening Part 1`
2 Listen and Select (graphic)	The same as Listen and Select, but in this section the options are pictures, not words. 🎧 *listen twice*	`Listening Part 1`
3 Extended Listening	A longer recording. This might be: • an interview • a business presentation • a conversation 🎧 *listen twice*	• up to 6 multiple-choice questions • 3 or 4 options to click on for each question (A, B, C or D) `Listening Part 4`

Reading and Language Knowledge questions

Question type	You will read	Your task
1 Read and Select	One of the following: • a notice • a diagram • a label • a memo or letter	• a short multiple-choice question • 3 or 4 options to click on for each question (A, B, C or D) Reading Part 1, Section 1
2 Extended Reading	• a longer text (about 300–400 words)	• up to 6 multiple-choice questions • 3 or 4 options to click on for each question (A, B, C or D) Reading Part 1, Section 3 Reading Part 2, Section 5
3 Multiple-choice gap fill	• a text with up to 6 spaces (about 75–150 words)	• short multiple-choice questions • click on the correct word for each space • 3 or 4 options to click on for each space (A, B, C or D) Reading Part 2, Section 2
4 Open gap fill	• a text with up to 10 spaces (about 75–150 words)	• type the correct word in each space • there are no options to choose from Reading Part 1, Section 4 Reading Part 2, Section 3
5 Gapped sentences	• sentences with a space	• click on the correct word or phrase for each space • 4 options to click on for each space (A, B, C or D) Reading Part 1, Section 2 Reading Part 2, Section 4

How does it work?

The Computer Test changes the level of the questions according to the answers you give. If you answer questions correctly, the computer will choose more difficult ones. If you answer questions incorrectly, the computer will give you easier ones. This is called adaptive testing. The CD ROM which accompanies this book contains BULATS test questions from Cambridge ESOL. It will help you become familiar with the way the test works and the type of questions you might have to do in the real test. (These questions are not adaptive.)

Points to remember
• You can listen to each of the Listening tasks twice.
• You can change any of your answers as often as you like until you click to move to the next section. When you move to the next section, you cannot go back.
• You should never leave a question unanswered. If you don't know the answer, guess.

Preparation tips
• For further practice, visit the BULATS website: www.BULATS.org.
• You can try out another sample BULATS Computer Test before you take the real test yourself.

Answer key and recording scripts

Listening Part 1 Practice (pages 6–7)

Listening skills practice (picture questions)

2 Product C
   a increased again
   b done well
   c to be
   d when
   e next month

3 Office A
   a not next
   b any more
   c thought about
   d post
   e now

Test practice (picture questions)

4 A
5 C

Test practice (text/written questions)

7 A
8 C
9 B
10 B

Recording scripts

🎧2 Question 2: Which product is the company going to[1] launch?
And finally, I'm delighted to tell you that this year our sales have been very good. Sales of photo printers have increased again[2], laptops have also done well[2], and we expect the HR4M digital camera to be[3] a great success when[3] it goes on to the market next month[3].

> [1] It must be a new product. It isn't on the market now.
> [2] This tells you they aren't new products.
> [3] These things tell us he is talking about the future.

🎧3 Question 3: Which is the correct picture of the new office?
F: What's happened to the office? I couldn't find the photocopier this morning.
M: We made some changes while you were on holiday.
F: I noticed!
M: Yes, it's not next[1] to the coffee machine any more[1] – it was too crowded sometimes during coffee breaks. We thought about[2] reception, but that would be too noisy.
F: So it's in the post room now[3].

> [1] The old situation.
> [2] Thinking about something is not the same as doing it.
> [3] The current situation.

🎧4 Question 4: Which graph shows the correct production figures?
M: I'm glad to see that production has improved. What happened at the beginning of the year?
F: Well, we had a few problems with the machines, but at least it didn't fall like it did last year[1].
M: Yes, that was a disaster. Maybe next year we can start the year with an increase[2] for a change.
F: That would be a nice surprise!

> [1] Production fell last year, not this year.
> [2] This is talking about next year, not this year.

🎧5 Question 5: What date does the sales conference start?
M: When's the sales conference going to be this year? Is it on the 14th like last year?
F: Well, we had trouble getting all the speakers on the day we wanted – the 14th[1] – so we've decided on the 18th[2] now. We're lucky to have a conference at all. Nearly everywhere was booked. I think it was the tenth place[3] I phoned that was able to help us.

> [1] This tells you why it can't be the 14th.
> [2] This tells you the date.
> [3] This is not related to dates.

🎧6 Question 7: Who is the sales person talking to on the phone?
We've had a lot of complaints about this product. I don't think we should be offering it to our customers. You're managing this account so, if you agree, I'd like to contact the suppliers and cancel the order.

> Would you say this to a customer or a supplier?

🎧7 Question 8: What does the announcer say about the flight to Málaga?
This is the last call[1] for all passengers travelling on Flight RA 434 to Málaga. Please proceed immediately[1] to Gate 22, repeat Gate 22, where your flight is ready to board[1]. We apologise for[2] the change in gate numbers. This is due to a technical problem with a previous flight[3].

> [1] These expressions all tell us that the flight is soon.
> [2] Apologies are often for delays, but not in this case.
> [3] The problem is not with the Málaga flight.

🎧8 Question 9: What is the manager going to do tomorrow?
F: It's going to be a busy day tomorrow. We've got to get ready for the big presentation – we'll discuss that in the afternoon[1]. We've also got that strategy meeting soon. Can we talk about that in the morning[2], Mike?
M: Sure. What time?
F: Well, I'll be making[3] some important phone calls first thing[3], so shall we say about 11.00?

> [1] 'Discuss', not 'give'.
> [2] 'Talk about', not 'attend'.
> [3] Making calls in the morning.

🎧9 **Question 10: Who is the man on the phone going to meet today?**
This is a message for Paul. Paul, I'm really sorry, but something's come up, a meeting I have to go to. It's all very last minute and I just can't get out of it. I know this isn't the first time, but, as I said, it's really important. He might be signing a big contract with us[1] and I have to take him out[1] for a meal somewhere. Don't worry, we can have our meeting on Friday[2].

> [1] 'He' and 'him' are the person he is meeting.
>   A client might sign a contract.
> [2] This meeting will take place on Friday, not today.

Listening Part 1 Test (pages 8–11)

1	C	2	A	3	C	4	A	5	A
6	B	7	B	8	B	9	A	10	C

Recording script
🎧 10

Part 1. Questions 1–10.
You will hear 10 short recordings. For questions 1 to 10, circle one letter A, B or C for the correct answer. You will hear each recording twice.

Question 1. Which pie chart is correct?
As consumers eat out more and buy more ready-made convenience foods to eat at home, pizza consumption has grown dramatically, especially home deliveries which have grown by about a third since 1998. Most consumers get their pizzas from supermarkets, accounting for just over half of all pizza sales. At second position with a quarter share of the market are home deliveries. Restaurant pizzas have the smallest share of about 20%.

Question 2. Which of the products ordered are out of stock?
This is David Marshall, Office Furniture. It's about your order TH89100, We've despatched your desks today, but I'm afraid we've had a problem in our warehouse and the chairs won't be ready to send until tomorrow. There's also a delay with the filing cabinets, which have been so popular that we've sold out. We're now awaiting another delivery. Sorry for the inconvenience this causes. Please call if you need to. Bye.

Question 3. Which piece of equipment needs to be repaired?
F: Hello, technician's department.
M: Hi, Jan. Thanks for fixing my laptop yesterday. I've got another problem now. The photocopier keeps jamming paper, and I think it's overheating. I'm printing off copies from file on the printer at the moment, but it takes much longer. Could you come and take a look?
F: OK. I'll come over this afternoon.

Question 4. What is the first thing that the speaker usually does at work?
A driver meets me at my home at about seven to take me to work. Once I'm there, I start the day by making phone calls. Then I check my schedule and bring myself up-to-date for site visits. Most of the visits are to meet with construction people, from site managers to sales staff.

Question 5. Which chart shows the correct figures?
The mood is optimistic amongst ad agencies now emerging from the slump their industry has seen over recent years, especially as the spend on TV advertising has picked up again. Newspapers don't fare so well, and there is still some work to be done in bringing their share of total European spend back up to the levels of two years ago, but on the internet, the increase in advertising revenue remains steady.

Question 6. What is the latest news about Peterson's?
One of the largest meat product manufacturers, Peterson's, has been rescued from the brink of collapse. The company, which called in the receivers at the beginning of this year, has been bought up by Crawley Foods, a new organisation established by joint MDs Nick Letwin and Dean Yates.

Question 7. What is notable about the consumption of eggs by 17- to 24-year-olds?
Although they account for only 9% of all eggs consumed, most interestingly, the 17 to 24 age group, both males and females, are one of the few age groups to have increased their egg consumption over the past year, by almost 8%. The largest decline is by adults aged from 25 to 34 years old.

Question 8. What was causing a problem for shopkeepers?
New colour-coded strips on the labels of Carson's drinks will differentiate the variants in their fruit drinks ranges. Carson's have just altered the look of their brand by updating the shape and size of the bottles they use, and now the colour coding on the bottles and on the outer packaging will help identify the products more easily. Retailers had complained that previously, the different products in the range could not be quickly distinguished.

Question 9. What is the speaker's view of the housing market?
I feel that the cyclical nature of the housing market is no longer as severe or dramatic. There aren't the peaks and troughs that there once were, just mild waves of interest and demand. There are observers who are waiting for the market to fall off a cliff edge, and just won't believe that it's not going to.

Question 10. What does the speaker criticise about the website?
The Office Point uses the web to promote its wide range of products and services, and their site does the job perfectly competently. I especially appreciated the way that the contact details and opening hours of the stores are prominently displayed on each page. The only thing I found slightly unsatisfactory was that the style of the home page isn't reflected through the rest of the site.

Listening Part 2 Practice (pages 12–13)

Listening skills practice
1 2 printer paper
   3 tomorrow
   4 0343 423 7373
2 a reference number
   b warehouse
   c containers
   d February
   e representatives
   f financial manager
   g Wednesday
   h 17 people
   i specifications

> Did you have a problem with this number? Be careful with numbers which are easily confused such as 13 and 30; 14 and 40.

> Pay attention to plurals.

Test practice
1 cleaning
2 computer virus
3 reference number
4 warehouse
5 labour
6 Project Finance
7 9.00/9 o'clock
8 New York trip

🎧 11

a If you give me the reference number of the invoice, I can check the amount for you.

b We'd like to arrange delivery to our warehouse near Paris.

c We expected four containers of goods, but we have only received three of them.

d I'm afraid we won't be able to complete the project until February at the earliest.

e One of our representatives will visit you with some samples.

f I suggest you contact the financial manager if you have any questions about the payment method.

g I'll be out of the office until Wednesday.

h There will be about 17 people at the presentation.

i What are the exact specifications of the product?

🎧 12 **Conversation 1. Questions 1–4.**

Look at the message below. You will hear a man leaving a message for your colleague about a delivery problem.

Hello. This is a message for Alain. It's Pete Thompson at FX Transport. I'm just ringing about the cleaning supplies you asked for last week. Look, I'm really sorry, but I'm afraid we've had a computer virus here and we've lost some of our customer order details. When you get this message, could you call us? We need to check the product reference number. Our number's 0203 4533 3455. Oh, I almost forgot. We delivered to your warehouse last time – not the office building. Is that the same for this order? Let me know. Look forward to hearing from you.

🎧 13 **Conversation 2. Questions 5–8.**

Look at the notes below. You will hear a man talking to a colleague about a meeting they are going to attend.

M: Hello, Sally? It's Matt.

F: Hi, Matt. How are you?

M: Fine. Listen, I'm calling you about the project meeting tomorrow – you remember I asked you to bring those figures on the raw material costs? Well, could you also bring your figures for labour costs, too?

F: Of course. Is there a problem?

M: No, no. It's just that someone from the bank – their Project Finance Manager – is going to be at the meeting and he's asked for a full cost breakdown.

F: No problem. I'll bring the figures you asked for. The meeting's at 9.30, isn't it?

M: Yes, but could you get there at 9.00 so I can look at those figures myself before we start?

F: OK. See you then. Bye.

M: Oh, sorry, Sally, I almost forgot. Have you got a copy of that report on your New York trip? You promised me a copy, remember?

F: Sure. Sorry about that. I'll make a note to bring it.

M: Thanks. Bye Sally.

F: Bye.

Listening Part 2 Test (pages 14–15)

Conversation 1

11 Financial advisor/adviser

12 Diploma in Accountancy

13 Business Services

14 (the) South(-)West

Conversation 2

15 plastic sheeting

16 (the) middle of March / mid March

17 container

18 (the) customer care

Conversation 3

19 (a) Field Representative

20 publisher(s)

21 15% / fifteen percent of sales

22 (the) 1(st) (of) April / April (the) 1(st) / 1/4 / 4/1

Recording script

🎧 14 **Part 2. Questions 11–22.**

You will hear three conversations. Fill in the numbered spaces, using the information you hear. You will hear each conversation once only.

Conversation 1. Questions 11–14.

Look at the form below. You will hear a phone call from a magazine reader to the magazine asking for franchising company prospectuses. You have 20 seconds to look at the form.

Now listen and complete the form.

F: OK, Mr Tyson. Some details about yourself first – your postcode and house number?

M: SN2 8BY, number ten.

F: Right. And what do you do?

M: At the moment, I'm a financial advisor.

F: OK. Do you have any special skills or qualifications?

M: I have a Diploma in Accountancy.

F: Right. Now about the franchise companies – if you tell me what kind you are considering, I can select the relevant prospectuses to send you.

M: OK. I'm most interested in Business Services companies – I noticed a few in your magazine.

F: Yes, there are some good ones. And what area of the country are you looking in?

M: I'm just about to move down from the Midlands to the South West, so that's the area I want to find out about.

F: Fine. I'll post them out to you today.

M: Thanks, bye.

F: Bye.

Conversation 2. Questions 15–18.

Look at the message below. You will hear a phone message from a supply company. You have 20 seconds to look at the form.

Now listen and complete the form.

Hello, this is a message for Emily Chung from Sam Webster of SW Packaging Supplies. It's about your order for rolls of plastic sheeting. Unfortunately, we won't be able to supply your goods at the time that we agreed. I'm afraid the earliest we can deliver will be the middle of March. We've been let down by the manufacturers – we're still awaiting the arrival of a container from them which was due in January. We are very sorry for any inconvenience this causes, and if there is any problem with the revised delivery schedule, please call customer care on 01424 797999.

Conversation 3. Questions 19–22.

Look at the notes below. You will hear a phone call between an employment agent and his client about a job vacancy. You have 20 seconds to look at the form.

Now listen and complete the form.

M: Hello Judy, it's Frank Geddy from the employment agency. I've got a post you might be interested in.
F: Great. What is it?
M: It's a vacancy for a Field Representative with a company called Campbell and Ross.
F: Right, what kind of business is it?
M: Campbell and Ross are publishers – their headquarters are in Oxford.
F: OK. And what sort of terms are they offering?
M: As well as the basic salary, you'd get 15% of sales, plus pension and long holidays – they sell mainly to schools.
F: Right. So when do they want applications in by?
M: Er … the advert only came in on Monday, so you should have plenty of time … yes, you've got until the 1st of April. They want your CV and covering letter.
F: Fine, I'll come over and pick up the details.
M: OK, see you then.
F: Bye.

Listening Part 3 Practice (pages 16–17)

Listening skills practice

Space 2: standards (to make you think of the quality control department – F)
Answer: Person 1 is C (sales and marketing department)

Space 3: complaints (to make you think of customer services – B)
Space 4: produce (to make you think of the production department – G)
Answer: Person 2 is F (quality control department)

Test practice

Person 3: A (delivery department)
Person 4: D (accounts department)
Person 5: G (production department)

Recording scripts

🎧 **15** *Person 1:* I know we're working hard to increase output and improve standards, but it doesn't really matter how good our products are, or how many we make, if the customers aren't interested in buying them. <u>We make sure that customers know our products exist, see them in magazines and newspapers, and so on.</u>

> *Answer: Making customers aware of a company's products is part of sales and marketing.*

🎧 **16** *Person 2:* We don't get that many complaints these days, but when we do, it's probably my responsibility. If a customer receives one of our products that doesn't work, OK I didn't produce it myself, but <u>I, or someone in my department should have noticed the problem before it left the factory; it should have been checked.</u>

> *Answer: Quality control is the department which checks for mistakes.*

🎧 **17** *Person 3:* I've been with this company for twenty years and I've seen a lot of changes. We used to write everything on paper – we were always filing things and if you lost a piece of paper, well! Now we <u>log everything on computers</u>[1]. <u>We know the address we're going to and the orders we're taking there</u>[2]. Of course, we still use paper. Everything gets printed, but nowadays you can't lose it!

> [1] *Distractor for IT department.*
> [2] *Answer: Who needs to know where they are taking products? The delivery department staff.*

Person 4: I suppose we're the department that no one thinks about until we make a mistake and then <u>they're straight on the phone to us</u>[1]. I can understand that, I mean people don't like to be underpaid, do they? <u>If you work hard all week, you want to get what you've earned</u>[2].

> [1] *Distractor: People often phone customer services when angry.*
> [2] *Answer: Who pays people? The accounts department staff.*

Person 5: We've just invested some money in new equipment for this department, so, in the long term our <u>manufacturing output</u>[1] should increase. The problem is that right now, everyone's being <u>re-trained</u>[2] on our new machines, so we can't meet the orders as quickly as usual. I keep telling Sales to let the customers know, but I'm sure there have been <u>complaints</u>[3].

> [1] *Answer: Who needs to manufacture things? The production department staff.*
> [2] *Distractor for training department.*
> [3] *Distractor for the customer services department.*

Listening Part 3 Test (page 18)

Section 1

23 A	**24** G	**25** B	**26** H	**27** E

Section 2

28 C	**29** D	**30** E	**31** B	**32** A

Recording script

🎧 **18** **Part 3. Section 1. Questions 23–27.**

You will hear five people talking about changes that companies have made. As you listen to each one, decide the area in which each company has made changes. Choose your answer from the list A to I, and write the correct letter in the space provided. You will hear the five pieces once only. You have 20 seconds to read the list A to I.

Now listen to the example.

Two years ago, Galway Electronics faced a worryingly high level of staff turnover. The Chief Executive was convinced that the key to lowering this was job satisfaction. So production on an assembly line, with everybody doing just one task, has now been replaced by teamwork, where team members carry out all the tasks necessary to produce finished goods. The outcome has been a significant fall in staff turnover.

They are talking about organisation of work activities, so you write 'I' as your answer.

Question 23. Person 1.

Pidgley Foods is so small that it's almost invisible, in comparison with the big players in its sector. This has an impact on sales, as consumers tend to opt for better-known brands, regardless of quality. Since last year the company has been making a concerted effort to raise the profile of the Pidgley brand, through a combination of press releases and paid advertising, and it's gained many new customers.

Question 24. Person 2.

Whiteridge is an insurance group that's achieving steady growth. Its senior managers believe the firm can only succeed by tapping the knowledge and ideas of the employees. To that end, the company has introduced a system to ensure that the whole workforce is kept informed of what's going on, and everyone is encouraged to make comments or present ideas – by email, anonymously in a suggestions box, or by other means.

Question 25. Person 3.

Some of this country's best-known brands of sweets and chocolates are produced by Foremost Confectionery. However, the group has suffered from a lack of innovation, and stagnating sales. To turn this around, Foremost has – for the first time – embarked on an extensive programme of market research, to find out how new brands can be made to match changed consumer preferences. Their hope is that they haven't left it too late.

Question 26. Person 4.

The Chatham Construction Group used to spend a great deal of time and money on tendering for new projects. The situation has improved, however, as the group now attempts to 'lock in' clients. One way is by providing top-quality work. In addition, Chatham aims to develop long-term relationships, by offering additional, ongoing services, such as maintenance and technical support. As a result, Chatham has a high proportion of repeat business.

Question 27. Person 5.

When John Cousins, the founder of Cousins Financial Services, stepped down, his place as Chief Executive was taken by the dynamic Stephanie Reade. She decided to change the male-dominated nature of the company, and to recruit far more women and staff from a range of ethnic backgrounds. The successful implementation of this policy has had the effect of drawing in a variety of new customers, and turnover has soared.

Part 3. Section 2. Questions 28–32.

You will hear five people giving advice about what to do before signing a contract. As you listen to each one, decide what advice each speaker gives. Choose your answer from the list A to I, and write the correct letter in the space provided. You will hear the five pieces once only. You have 20 seconds to read the list A to I.

Now listen to the example.

Remember that legal advisers are there to get the best deal for their clients. And they can be ruthless. Their priorities may be different from yours. Before adding your signature, you should always check in detail any contracts drawn up on your behalf to make sure you are aware of everything contained in them, and that you are completely happy with all the demands and offers made.

Their advice is to always check the contracts written by your own lawyers, so you write 'I' as your answer.

Question 28. Person 1.

After reading the contract, consider if the offer being presented meets your needs. If not, contact the other party directly and say that you'd still like to do business, but not on the terms of this contract, as there are some points that still need discussion. You can always put the blame on their legal advisers if you are worried about offending them.

Question 29. Person 2.

When you sit down to read the contract, it is a good idea to ask other people with you to leave the room or to keep quiet whilst you go through it, taking as much time as you need. If you are distracted when you check the finer details of each section, you may miss crucial points that you will only be aware of when it's too late to re-negotiate the terms of the deal.

Question 30. Person 3.

Being realistic, you're not likely to get everything you want, so be ready to accommodate some of the other party's needs. You may have to move a little from your original position, but don't see that as losing. Of course, there will be points that you can't give way on, but there is always some space for compromise.

Question 31. Person 4.

I was given some very good advice once by a lawyer friend: always have a pen and paper with you as you read through any contract. As you read each paragraph, write down in brief and in your own words what you think the main points are. Legal documents can be hard to understand, so it helps if you can refer to your own words.

Question 32. Person 5.

Prior to reading the contract, prepare yourself by writing down what you think you have agreed to in discussions, and what you want to see in the contract. Don't let the other party's lawyers decide which things have to be negotiated – start from your own agenda, not theirs. Use these preparatory notes to remind yourself of your priorities when you review their offer.

Listening Part 4 Practice (pages 19–20)

Listening skills practice

1	A	2	C	3	B	4	B

Test practice

1	A	2	B	3	A	4	C

Recording scripts

🎧 19

> The answers are highlighted in blue.

Interviewer(I): Today I'm talking to Paul Green, one of the most successful retailers in this country. Paul, <u>when did you start in business</u>[1]?

Paul Green (PG): Like most students I had a summer job. I worked in a factory putting plastic toys in cereal boxes, but <u>I got my first proper job</u>[2] after I graduated. I saw an advertisement in the …

I: And how did you get into management?

PG: <u>My degree was in business studies</u>[3] so I applied to join a company at junior management level. My career really made progress when <u>I was headhunted to M&T</u>[4], the retail chain. They called me one day when I was …

I: What's the best advice you've ever had in business?

PG: <u>A colleague once told me</u>[5] that if you give the customers what they <u>want</u>[6], you will succeed in business. I think high sales are more important than low costs, although I know not everyone agrees …

I: You are known as a strong leader. What qualities does that require?

PG: Above all you must be willing[7] to make big decisions – even if your team doesn't agree[8] with them – and keep to them. It's no good changing your mind.

I: And now what plans do you have for …

> 1 *Notice how you can follow the questions.*
>
> 2 *This is the start of a business career (not a summer job).*
>
> 3 *He had studied business.*
>
> 4 *This was not his first management job.*
>
> 5 *Not the same as 'talk to your colleagues'.*
>
> 6 *want = need*
>
> 7 *If you are 'willing', you are prepared.*
>
> 8 *This is not the same as 'listen to your team'.*

🎧 **20**

Good afternoon everyone. As you know, I'm here to talk about the work my company does. We offer a range of assistance to companies expanding their operations internationally[1], including franchising and joint ventures. I'll say more about this later, but, basically, the help we give is mainly practical – transport and legal services, and so on. We don't handle the financial[2] side of things and, although we have many contacts in that area, training[2] and recruitment are areas we prefer to leave to local specialists.

I'd like to start by discussing franchising. Although the profits are smaller than when you build your own factory and employ your own staff, it is certainly safer to start with some kind of franchise agreement. A local person will operate their own factory to produce and sell your products so you have none of the set-up costs of building a new plant. It will still be your product, of course, but the risks are shared[3] between you. How can we help? Well, one of the services my company can provide is legal help[4] with franchise contracts between you and the local business person, once you have made contact[5] with someone suitable.

Another strategy worth considering is a joint venture: a 50–50[6] investment between you and another company. What are the advantages and disadvantages of this? Well, at first the investment costs are shared equally with your local partner, but you do, in the long term, have risks: the most obvious is one side wanting to break the agreement for some reason. Successful joint ventures[7] can take time to establish and we can …

> 1 *Another word for 'abroad'.*
>
> 2 *Financial help and training are not offered.*
>
> 3 *There is a risk, but it is shared.*
>
> 4 *This refers to legal help, not legal costs.*
>
> 5 *You have to find a partner.*
>
> 6 *This doesn't mean 50% as in the question.*
>
> 7 *Successful joint ventures can take time.*

Listening Part 4 Test (pages 21–23)

Section 1

| **33** | B | **34** | A | **35** | B | **36** | C | **37** | B | **38** | C |

Section 2

| **39** | C | **40** | C | **41** | C | **42** | B | **43** | C | **44** | A |

Section 3

| **45** | B | **46** | A | **47** | A | **48** | B | **49** | C | **50** | A |

Recording script

🎧 **21**

Part 4. Section 1. Questions 33–38.

You will hear a college lecturer talking about the contribution of production and marketing to achieving business aims. For questions 33–38, circle one letter A, B or C for the correct answer. You will hear the talk twice. You have 20 seconds to read the questions.

Now you will hear the talk.

We've been looking at what companies need to do in order to stay in business and achieve their goals, and today I'll give you a short introduction to the roles of production and marketing.

It was Henry Ford, the American car manufacturer, who introduced mass production, and changed the way decisions were made about production. Rather than having skilled workers using machines to make things, he had machines using workers. He stood outside the production process, analysed it, and took decisions in principle about how it should work, instead of having production workers making decisions on an ad hoc basis. And he increased productivity, though only up to a point.

These days, the drawbacks of that approach are more apparent. For example, a shoe factory brought in a consultant, and he turned the whole thing on its head. He said the workers, not the managers, were the 'experts' on production, because they were the ones who were actively involved in it. So he had them do what he called the 'walk'. They literally walked round the factory, following the shoe through the manufacturing process. This means how far all the materials travel in total from start to finish, from one department to the next, and so on.

Then the consultant told them to forget about the production manager, and to redesign the production process in small sections where everything was done from start to finish, rather than separate departments in which everyone did the same thing. They did – and it worked. The production manager was amazed because with this new approach to space, the quantity of shoes produced per worker went up considerably.

A car factory with a serious problem of quality took a similar step, by handing responsibility for quality control over to the production workers. Again, things improved considerably. The input of supplies coming in was the same, but the process improved. Things were quicker, more responsive, so the factory could work more effectively to order, and keep less stock. Also, when errors did occur, they were spotted sooner.

The choice of production method has an impact on production costs, of course. But however good your product, you need to sell it, and marketing is another essential business tool. It's been defined as the use of innovation to change sales habits. Here's an example of how marketing can be used.

A well-known ice cream company has been very successful by virtue of its product. They decided to launch in this country against very stiff competition. Existing brands had already covered the normal high street distribution possibilities, so this company chose to fight on the basis of having a product that was unquestionably, and invariably, the best available, rather than by offering the widest choice or the most attractive cost to the consumer.

They also built up the idea of exclusivity, by opening just a few outlets, in upmarket areas of major cities. The packaging, too, was designed to reflect the image they wanted to convey. Above all, they relied on word of mouth by a small number of exclusive customers. They advertised selectively, just in smart magazines, alongside ads for perfume or jewellery. This was a very innovative approach to marketing an everyday product like ice cream, and it was a resounding success.

Now you will hear the talk again.

Part 4. Section 2. Questions 39–44.
You will hear a radio interview with Simon Cartier, the owner of a chain of clothing shops. For questions 39 to 44, circle one letter A, B or C for the correct answer. You will hear the interview twice. You have 20 seconds to read the questions.

Now you will hear the interview.

F: Simon Cartier's a prime example of someone succeeding through never giving up. When one business failed, he started his next venture immediately. Simon, let's start from the beginning when you first left your employment to become an entrepreneur. How did that happen?
M: I'd been an accountant for a chain of clothing stores for ten years, when it was taken over by the huge Davidia Group. They didn't want the company, and took action to ensure it ceased trading. Several of the managers set up on their own, and I admired their operation, and was envious of the large amount of money that they were making. I decided then that I wanted to do the same.
F: So how did you get the finances to start that first company?
M: I was lucky – my brother, Jack Cartier, lost his job at around that same time, and he received a payout. Unfortunately, what I had managed to save over the years had gone, so I persuaded him to put his money into starting our own clothing operation, *The Outfit*. That was in 1980. I was able to buy my brother out in 1987, and at the same time a venture capital group took a 10% share.
F: And then there was a recession which finished your business.
M: Yes.
F: But then you started your second clothing operation, *Massive Stores*. Was the concept for that similar to the original one?
M: No. Whereas my original company focused on the luxury end of the market, I needed to move to the other end of the scale. I considered retailing clothing for special purposes like sports, or uniforms, that kind of thing, but it demanded huge loans from banks for stock. Discount retail was the perfect answer because of the fast turnover of stock that was possible.
F: I see. And when you started up for the second time, it must have been easier – you knew the people in the industry, which must have helped?
M: Well, it wasn't that so much, it was that they knew me. That was a great benefit. Suppliers that I had used trusted me, and liked what I was doing, so were happy to supply enough stock for me to get started. Also, my landlord allowed me to pay my first month's rent in arrears.
F: And the business took off quickly – turnover is now £120 million. How involved in the day-to-day running of the business are you now?

M: Well, you've got to know your own limits. As the company's grown, I've brought more people in. I've recruited a buyer who really knows what he is doing, and an excellent finance director – that's my area of expertise, but I wanted to spend more time on finding, acquiring and opening new stores. With a current target of 20 to 40 further stores per year, it's a full-time job!
F: And do you think you might retire soon?
M: I've heard so many stories about successful business people who've given it all up and gone golfing or away on their yacht, but then 18 months later they come back and start again. It's in the blood, it's what they enjoy doing. Business challenges me and stimulates me. I get a kick out of doing deals and negotiating with people that I just couldn't get anywhere else.
F: Right. Well, thank you very much, Simon Cartier.

Now you will hear the interview again.

Part 4. Section 3. Questions 45–50.
You will hear Diana Warren, a business consultant, giving a talk on how she set up her business consultancy. For questions 45–50, circle one letter A, B or C for the correct answer. You will hear the talk twice. You have 20 seconds to read the questions.

Now you will hear the talk.

When I decided to strike out on my own after 25 years as an employee, I thought about all kinds of business ideas, but then realised my own CV held the answer. My professional experience, knowledge and specialist understanding constituted a business opportunity with great potential.

Once I had decided to become a consultant, the first thing I did was take a detailed look at what skills and knowledge I could offer. What had I learnt in my experience that I could sell to others? I listed all the projects I'd undertaken, what part I played in them, what the outcome was and what I'd learned from them. That took some time, but it gave me the starting point for when I came to consider potential clients.

But before doing that, I had to consider whether I had the requisite personal attributes to succeed as a consultant: self-motivation, good interpersonal skills and self-confidence. I felt quite happy about the first two – much of the work I'd previously done would have been impossible without them. But I found that in the early days of the consultancy I had to fake the confidence. After all, it was all new for me and I was uncertain of what I could do. I just convinced myself that the client was probably more unsure than I was, and carried on as if I had all the confidence in the world.

So once I had a clear idea of what I could offer as a consultant, I investigated whether my skills and knowledge would be valued in the marketplace. To successfully make this assessment, you must understand what is going on in the world around you. Most importantly, you should offer skills to businesses in fields which are increasingly popular and where the skills you have are in short supply. So I looked at economic forecasts, business trends and all the latest approaches to management.

After considering all these factors, I went about selling my 'product'. I found it best to be as specialist as possible, because a neat package of specific skills is far more attractive to customers than a list of generalised expertise.

When it came to marketing, my start-up budget didn't stretch to launching an advertising campaign in the general or sector-specific journals. I started the process by networking intensively. I contacted all my friends, family, acquaintances, ex-business colleagues, everyone in my address book, and told them what I was doing. This yielded most of my early enquiries, and in fact my first client was my previous employer!

Another way I promoted my new consultancy was to get articles published in leading journals in my chosen sectors. This cost me little but time. I didn't get masses of leads from my first few appearances in print, but such promotion did my professional reputation no harm, and I often re-use the material on my website, in mail-outs to clients and in new business presentations.

Implemented with enthusiasm, commitment and care, these steps led to a successful and rewarding new business with very low start-up costs.

Now you will hear the talk again.

Reading and Language Knowledge Part 1, Section 1
Practice (pages 26–27)

Practice exercises

Synonyms

2 a   **3** d   **4** c   **5** b

Here is a list of useful synonyms:

> I apologise = I am sorry / I'm afraid
> call off = cancel
> meeting = appointment
> at short notice = at the last minute
> we regret to inform you = we're sorry to tell you
> no longer in stock = unavailable
> second-to-none = best
> field of business = line of business
> enquiries = questions
> relevant = correct
> away from the office = not at my/the desk

Make a list of synonyms in a vocabulary notebook.

Identifying why a person is writing

Here are the expressions matched with the reasons for writing. The underlined expressions are the key words.

1 Providing explanations
  d The late arrival <u>was the result of</u> a train strike.
  g <u>Due to</u> a problem with our supplier, all deliveries will be delayed.

2 Offering to do something
  e <u>If we can help you in any way, please do not hesitate to ask.</u>
  l <u>We would be delighted to</u> discuss this in more detail.

3 Requesting something
  c <u>I would be grateful if you could</u> send me a copy.
  f <u>I'd really appreciate it if</u> you sent me a new price list.

4 Informing someone
  a <u>I am pleased to tell you that</u> your order is ready.
  i <u>I have to advise you that</u> your payment is late.

5 Complaining about something
  b <u>I'm afraid this is not acceptable.</u>
  j <u>I am extremely dissatisfied with</u> the product I bought.

6 Enquiring about something
  h <u>I'm writing to ask you</u> when it will be ready for collection.
  k <u>Could you let me know</u> how often you deliver?

Look out for examples of this type of language in your business letters and emails.

Test practice

The correct answers are underlined.

1 The Central Plaza Hotel offers Toronto's <u>biggest</u> fully-equipped business centre for meetings, conventions and other business needs. Ideal for the business traveller.

  The Central Plaza
  A offers the best facilities for business guests in Toronto.
  B is only recommended for business people.
  C <u>would suit large companies wishing to hold a conference.</u>

Biggest does not always mean best.

Not only business people.

2 Please ignore this email if you have already received the goods you requested on 7th March, otherwise contact us immediately by phone.

  What does this email tell you?

In other words: if your order has arrived, do nothing. If it hasn't, call us.

  A You need to telephone the company to tell them if your order has arrived.
  B <u>You don't need to reply to this email if your order has been delivered.</u>
  C You should email the company if you want to arrange a new delivery date.

3 <u>To qualify</u> for a 10% discount, <u>your order must exceed $5,000</u>. We <u>cannot</u> make an <u>exception</u>, even for <u>new customers</u>.

The key words in this message are underlined.

  What is this company's policy on discounts?
  A All new customers get a 10% discount on their orders.
  B <u>No customers can get a discount on orders of less than $5,000.</u>
  C New customers have to spend more than $5,000 on their first order.

4 *businessflightfinder.com* searches more than 200 different airlines to bring you the cheapest business flights on the web.

  businessflightfinder.com is
  A <u>an agency for budget business travel.</u>
  B a low-cost business airline.
  C an online guide to using the internet for travel.

What would you expect to buy from this company? Cheap tickets. Who finds cheap tickets? Agencies. (A)

Reading and Language Knowledge Part 1, Section 1
Test (pages 28–30)

51 C   **52** A   **53** A   **54** B   **55** A
56 B   **57** C

Reading and Language Knowledge Part 1, Section 2
Practice (pages 31–32)

Example: B

Keeping vocabulary records

2 All correct except:
  c The management are discussing ~~about~~ this problem.
  g When will you pay me ~~by~~ **for** the work I did last week?
  h Time for questions is included ~~to~~ **in** my presentation.

3 obtain: acquire, achieve (These words are all connected with the idea of getting something.)
offer: present, propose (These words are all connected with the idea of giving or suggesting something.)
improve: boost, further (These words are all connected with the idea of making something better.)

  a present (You present something to someone.)
  b achieve
  c boosted (This means increase in number, value or strength.)
  d acquired (*Acquire a reputation for …* is a strong collocation.)
  e proposes (Usually you offer something positive that people want. Propose is stating a plan to do something.)
  f further (*Further your career* is a strong collocation.)

Test practice

The correct answers are underlined.

1 Our new pocket PC is targeted .... the business traveller.
  A <u>at</u>   **B** on   **C** with   **D** to

> *'Aimed at' means the same thing.*

2 One of the .... to consumers of competition between companies is lower prices.
  A <u>benefits</u>   **B** advances   **C** improvements   **D** profits

> A benefits to consumers (but benefits of competition)
> B advances in e.g. technology = improvements
> C You can make improvements to products.

3 People are .... less on luxury goods than they were last year.
  A buying   **B** purchasing   **C** paying   **D** <u>spending</u>

> A You buy goods (no preposition).
> B You purchase goods (no preposition).
> C You pay for something.
> D This is the only one that goes with 'on'.

4 The management are .... a possible pension plan for the employees.
  A <u>discussing</u>   **B** talking   **C** thinking   **D** deciding

> A No preposition with 'discuss'.
> B We talk about things.
> C We think about things.
> D We decide on things.

5 Our market .... is declining. We've got to do something.
  A proportion   **B** section   **C** portion   **D** <u>share</u>

> *'Share' is the only collocation with 'market' in this group.*

6 In my report I've .... the sales figures you asked for.
  A involved   **B** contained   **C** <u>included</u>   **D** comprised

> A involved in something
> B 'Contain' means to have something inside itself (e.g. The box contained some books.).
> C You can include figures in a report.
> D 'Comprise' is like 'consist of' (e.g. His collection of cars comprised 27 Rolls-Royces.).

Reading and Language Knowledge Part 1, Section 2
Test (page 33)
58 B   **59** B   **60** D   **61** A   **62** D   **63** C

Reading and Language Knowledge Part 1, Section 3
Practice (pages 34–35)

Practice exercise

1 The correct answer is B. The text says that more and more companies find that the benefits, or results, of integrating fun and work (making work more enjoyable) are better relationships with colleagues and more money for the company.

2 A is true ('Changing attitudes doesn't happen overnight' means it takes a long time).
B is true ('showing your staff you trust them' has the same meaning).
C is not mentioned (the text says customers are important, but it doesn't say they are more important than staff).

3 A is not mentioned (the text says you should look for new staff who enjoy life. It doesn't compare with more experienced staff).
B is not mentioned.
C is true (the text says that 'training people to have fun is almost impossible').

4 A is mentioned ('applaud people's achievements' is a way of congratulating them).
B is not mentioned (the text says this is 'just one factor', meaning one of many. It doesn't say anywhere that it is the best).
C is mentioned ('Almost everyone enjoys the approval of their colleagues and friends').

Vocabulary

1	appropriate	7	raising
2	integrating	8	sociable
3	leads to	9	approach (to something)
4	attitudes	10	applaud (something)
5	vital	11	factor
6	valuable	12	approval (of something)

Test practice

1 A is not mentioned.
B is correct (the text says 'makes more money for the company').
C is not mentioned.

2 A is not mentioned.
B is false (the text talks about people who already have responsibility).
C is correct ('showing your staff you trust them').

3 A is false (you do this after hiring them).
B is correct ('recruiting one of the many people who enjoy life').
C is not mentioned.

4 A is correct (money 'is just one factor').
B is false (many people believe this, but it isn't true).
C is not mentioned (people enjoy the approval of colleagues and friends, but money isn't mentioned as a factor).

Reading and Language Knowledge Part 1, Section 3
Test (pages 36–37)

64 C **65** B **66** B **67** C **68** B **69** A

Reading and Language Knowledge Part 1, Section 4
Practice (pages 38–39)

Practice exercises

Articles

2 The (This is the second mention of this.)
3 the (This is a superlative – *the biggest*.)
4 a (This is a countable noun mentioned for the first time.)
5 an (This is a countable noun mentioned for the first time.)
6 the (There is only one of these, like the car industry, the steel industry, etc.)
7 the (*The* usually goes with *only*.)
8 an (There is more than one of these – did you remember about an with *a, e, i, o, u* words?)
9 a (This is a countable noun.)

some, any, much, many, this, that, these, those

1 any
2 much
3 many
4 Those
5 this
6 those
7 Some
8 these
9 This

Notes about the answers:
1 *Any* is often used with questions and negative sentences, e.g. *Have you got any money? I haven't got any money.*
2 *Much* is used with the question word *how* and with uncountable nouns – an uncountable noun is a noun which does not have a plural form and cannot be used with *a* or *one*, e.g. *work, money*.
3 *Many* is used with the question word *how* and with countable nouns like people and companies.
4 *Those* in this example is used like *the*. It is used with plurals.
5 *This* is used here to talk about a specific kind of work – the work we have already heard about at the beginning of the paragraph. It can't be *these* or *those* because they are used for plurals.
6 *Those* is used with plural countable nouns. It is used to describe something far from the speaker in distance, e.g. *Who are those people over there?*, and time. In this example *those* is used to talk about something plural in the past.
7 *Some* is used with countable nouns, e.g. *some people*, and uncountable nouns in positive sentences, e.g. *I've got some money.*
8 *These people* are the people we read about at the beginning of the sentence.
9 *This industry* is the service industry mentioned in the previous sentence.

> Don't confuse 'some' and 'any'!

Test practice

1 since (*Since* is used after a point in time in the past, e.g. *since 2001, since last year, since the company was founded.*)
2 most (If you see *the … + adjective*, the answer will be *most* – or *least*, but that does not fit in this context.)
3 the (*The* goes before a superlative form, e.g. *the fastest, the biggest.*)
4 this (*This* is used to refer back to something said earlier, in this case how people see you as a manager.)
5 by (*To be + verb + by* is a passive structure.)

> 'By' is often used with passives in this section.

Reading and Language Knowledge Part 1, Section 4
Test (page 40)

70 so **71** by **72** have **73** in **74** be

Reading and Language Knowledge Part 2, Section 1
Practice (pages 41–43)

Practice exercises

Sentence matching

2 e **3** f **4** a **5** h **6** d **7** c **8** g

Vocabulary: Modal verbs

2 c **3** f **4** d **5** a **6** b **7** g **8** e

Vocabulary: Useful expressions

1
a 1 **b** 7 **c** 4 **d** 8 **e** 2 **f** 6 **g** 3 **h** 5

2
1 features
2 run out of
3 assume
4 check
5 all-in-one
6 version
7 overall
8 prefer

Test practice

> The section of text which gives the answer is after each answer. Are they the same as you underlined?

1 B 'I think it's the most useful thing I own.'
(It can't be useful in only one situation if it's the most useful thing she owns.)
2 D 'music helps me unwind'
(*Relax* and *unwind* are synonyms. Synonyms can help you find the correct part of the text for your answer.)
3 A 'I've had three of these already, but none have been as good as I'd hoped.'
(*So far* is like saying *up to now* and *I've had three of these already* means *up to now* too. None have been very good, so we can assume she is disappointed.)
4 C 'I'd be happier without one of these.'
(Enjoyment and happiness are connected: if you don't enjoy something, you would be happier without it, or not doing it.)
5 A 'What I'd prefer is an all-in-one version.'
(*All-in-one* means many functions combined in one device.)
6 D 'I do a lot of travelling.'
(Travelling a lot is part of this woman's lifestyle.)

Reading and Language Knowledge Part 2, Section 1
Test (pages 44–45)

75 D   **76** C   **77** B   **78** D   **79** C
80 A   **81** B

Reading and Language Knowledge Part 2, Section 2
Practice (pages 46–47)

Practice exercises

Collocations
1 taken (A)
2 accepted (C)
3 further (B)
4 satisfy (B)
5 delivery (A)

> Check any other vocabulary from this exercise in your dictionary.

Vocabulary
The collocation is given in brackets.
1 result (in) (A)
2 influence (on) (C)
3 rate (of) (B)
4 expenditure (on) (D)
5 benefit (from) (C)
6 take part (in) (B)
7 shown (someone that) (B)
8 revealed (details) (D)
9 sum (of) (B)
10 quantity (of) (D)

Test practice
1 B (Only *impact* collocates with *make* and *on*, although *have an impact/an effect/an influence* are all possible collocations.)
2 A (Only *at no cost* is the correct collocation.)
3 D (*Take advantage of*, but *take part* in.)
4 C (*To prove to be* + adjective or noun is a common structure.)
5 C (Only *(in) the vast majority (of)* is a possible collocation.)

Reading and Language Knowledge Part 2, Section 2
Test (page 48)

82 C   **83** B   **84** A   **85** D   **86** B

Reading and Language Knowledge Part 2, Section 3
Practice (pages 49–50)

Practice exercises

which, that, who, where, when
b who   c when   d which / that

1 who
2 when (This could also be *while* meaning 'at the same time as'.)
3 which (Use *which*, not *that* after a comma.)
4 where (*An area* is used here like you might say *an area of London*.)
5 who (Mr Bennett gave the money to the schools, so it must be 'who'.)
6 which
7 who
8 which/that (The grocery business is a thing.)

> Sometimes more than one answer could be possible, e.g. which/that, but this is unusual. Take extra care to think about your answer if you think there is more than one possibility.

Prepositions with nouns and adjectives
2 acceptable to
3 benefit from
4 capable of (*Capable of* could also be followed by a noun, e.g. *He is capable of good work.*)
5 increase in (Nouns which describe rise and fall e.g. *a decrease* are often followed by *in*.)
6 familiar with
7 cooperate with (You always need at least two people or companies to cooperate with each other.)
8 depend on
9 participation in (This combination is followed here by the *-ing* form of a verb.)

Common mistakes
1 that (Remember: *that* or *which* can be used with things.)
2 few (We use *few* with countable nouns, e.g. *a few people*. We use *little* with uncountable nouns, e.g. *a little money*.)
3 than (This is a common form for comparing things.)
4 most (We use *the* + *most* + adjective to form superlatives with longer adjectives, e.g. *the most intelligent person*.)

> Remember to use 'the' with superlatives.

5 decrease (If you see the article *a*, *an* or *the*, the missing word must be a noun. Be careful to use the correct form of the noun.)
6 specialise (Remember that some verbs are followed by *to* + infinitive and some are followed by the *-ing* form, e.g. *I enjoy reading*.)
7 where (Remember: use *where* to talk about places.)
8 much (We use *much* with uncountable nouns, e.g. *energy*. We use *many* with countable nouns, e.g. *machines*.)

Linking words
1 I am writing to complain **because** the goods I ordered have not arrived.

> 'Because' tells us that the first half of the sentence is the result of the second half.

2 The company is going to expand into both India **and** China.

> 'And' adds one more piece of information.

3 **Although** it will be huge investment, we really must have that new machine.

> 'Although' contrasts two ideas. It's like saying 'It's expensive, but we must have it.'

4 We closed the old factory because it was becoming unprofitable. **Also** there were health and safety problems.

> Use 'also' to add more information. It's like 'and' but you can use it to start a new sentence.

5 We can't afford to spend more money on either IT **or** language training next year.

> Use 'or' when there is a choice between two ideas.

6 Demand has rocketed **so** we need to recruit 200 new workers.

> 'So' tells us that the second half of the sentence is the result of the first half.

Test practice

1. few (*Words* is plural so this must be an expression to describe a countable noun – *a little* only works with uncountable nouns, e.g. *a little money.*)
2. which/that (*Which* and *that* are often both possible.)
3. Since (If you see a present perfect tense being used, e.g. *Disney have said …*, you may need to use *for* or *since*. *For* is used with periods of time, e.g. *for ten years*, *for a long time*. *Since* is used with points in time, e.g. *since 2001*, *since January.*)
4. all (*at all* means *in any way*. It is a good idea to learn other expressions like this if you see them in texts, e.g. *at last* (in the end/finally), *at least* (the minimum), *at first.*)
5. capable (Do you remember this one from the practice exercises?)

Reading and Language Knowledge Part 2, Section 3
Test (page 51)

87	which/that	**88**	for	**89**	from
90	so/therefore	**91**	let		

Reading and Language Knowledge Part 2, Section 4
Practice (pages 52–53)

Practice exercises

Related words

increase: boost, grow, raise
plan: agenda, list, programme
dangerous: deadly, hazardous, lethal
manage: administer, run, supervise
improve: refurbish, renovate, restructure
employees: colleagues, subordinates, workforce
bill: account, invoice, receipt
check: inspect, monitor, verify

1. restructure (Refurbish and renovate are both used to describe improvements to property.)
2. invoice (You receive a receipt after you have paid for something. An account could be a bank account where you keep your money or a company account which is a system where a company can receive goods and services and pay for them later.)
3. inspect (To monitor something means to watch or check something, like inspect, but over a period of time to see how it develops; to verify something is to check or prove that facts are correct.)
4. programme (A list is a series of names or numbers e.g. a mailing list, a shopping list. An agenda is a kind of list, e.g. the items to be discussed in a meeting.)
5. grow (All three verbs mean 'more', but boost and raise must go before a noun, i.e. to boost/raise something.)
6. supervise (To administer is used to describe managing a company or organisation. To run means to be in charge of something such as a department in a company.)
7. hazardous (Deadly and lethal both describe things which can kill you e.g. a deadly poison or a lethal weapon – a gun.)
8. workforce (Colleagues are people we work with and subordinates are people with less authority or power than others in a company structure. A manager has subordinates.)

Choosing the correct definition

1 a	**2** a	**3** b	**4** a	**5** b	**6** b

Test practice

The correct answers are underlined.

1. In this job, I can do things the way I like and I really enjoy that . . . .
   - **A** dependence
   - **B** <u>autonomy</u>
   - **C** permission
   - **D** reliance

   > A This has the opposite meaning.
   > B This means freedom or independence.
   > C You give someone permission to do something or you get permission to do something from another person.

2. Moving the company makes good sense . . . . We'd be much closer to our customers.
   - **A** conveniently
   - **B** suitably
   - **C** reasonably
   - **D** <u>logistically</u>

   > A, B, and C all sound positive, but have no connection to logistics – the planning and organisation needed to make a plan work successfully.

3. I expect this company to develop into a major . . . . in the IT industry.
   - **A** actor
   - **B** member
   - **C** <u>player</u>
   - **D** component

   > A 'major player' is a strong collocation. A player is involved in competition such as games.

4. One of our suppliers was . . . . bankrupt last month.
   - **A** <u>declared</u>
   - **B** forced
   - **C** turned
   - **D** stated

   > 'Declared bankrupt' is a common collocation.

5. If we don't complete the work on time, there's a . . . . clause of $4,000 per day.
   - **A** reward
   - **B** consequence
   - **C** <u>penalty</u>
   - **D** fine

   > A This has the opposite meaning.
   > C This is a common collocation meaning a financial punishment in business, e.g. for being late completing a project.
   > D This is a financial punishment, e.g. from the police.

6. We increased production to meet the recent . . . . in demand.
   - **A** upside
   - **B** upgrade
   - **C** uplift
   - **D** <u>upturn</u>

   > Check any other vocabulary in your dictionary.

Reading and Language Knowledge Part 2, Section 4
Test (pages 54–55)

92 C	**93** C	**94** B	**95** C	**96** B	**97** A

Reading and Language Knowledge Part 2, Section 5
Practice (pages 56–57)

Practice exercise

1. **A** No. Finding oil is a costly process.
   B No. This is not mentioned in paragraph 1.
   C Yes. 'computer software searches for lost data' (lines 2–3) and 'Like oil, old data is there, waiting to be discovered' (lines 7–8).
   D No. This is not mentioned. The results of data mining can be valuable, but this is not mentioned in paragraph 1.

2. **A** No. This is not mentioned.
   B No. It 'needn't take forever' (lines 11–12) means it needn't take a lot of time.
   C Yes. You need computers and 'the latest software' (line 11).
   D No. This is not mentioned.

3. **A** No. The text does not say that this is a useful product.
   B Yes. 'incredibly detailed files on customers can be created, stored and used as the basis of the next marketing campaign' (lines 24–26). Planning strategy based on knowledge of customers is very useful.
   C No. Like A, this is not mentioned as a useful product.
   D No. We know what is popular with each customer, but it doesn't mention the market.

4. **A** No. 'This dominance may be at risk from newer companies' (lines 30–31) but there is no mention of older companies losing market share to new companies at the moment.
   B No. They need to data mine them: 'Nowhere is data mining more necessary than in old, established industries' (lines 27–28).
   C Yes. 'The information in them could be just what they need to stay on top' (lines 34–35).
   D No. This is not mentioned.

A closer look at the text

1
a searches for
b software (software is used on the computers used in data mining)
c customer profiles (a profile is a description of someone, including their character and habits)
d something helpful or useful; something that could give an advantage (over someone or something)

2
a 4   d 8   g 2
b 6   e 1   h 5
c 7   f 3

Reading and Language Knowledge Part 2, Section 5
Test (pages 58–59)

98 B   **99** D   **100** C   **101** B   **102** A   **103** B

Reading and Language Knowledge Part 2, Section 6
Practice (pages 60–61)

Practice exercises

Verb forms

2. are making (This must be present continuous because *we are* + verb + *at the moment* is describing a current situation.)
3. will open (*Next month* tells you this is a future form.)
4. had already launched (*Had already launching* is grammatically incorrect. The correct form is: *had* + *already* + past participle = past perfect tense.)
5. has just bought (*Have* not *be* is used with the present perfect. Also, *just* is sometimes used with perfect tenses.)
6. was established (*Established* is the past participle of *establish*. This is a past passive.)
7. need (*Need* is correct here because this is a first conditional sentence: *If* + present simple.)
8. plan (The present simple is often used for the future for things on a timetable or schedule.)

Mistakes with plurals

1. There are <u>a number of</u> possible **times** we could meet. *(These underlined expressions indicate a plural form.)*
2. This consultancy offers **advice** in financial matters.
3. This is <u>one of the</u> most important **pieces** of information in your contract.
4. There has been <u>a great deal of</u> investment in this project, but only a little progress. ✓ *(The underlined expression comes before singular or uncountable nouns.)*
5. The training budget can be reduced as <u>enough</u> **workers** have now been trained. *('Enough' is usually followed by the plural form of a word, unless the word is uncountable.)*
6. We have not had any monthly payments for the technical equipment we supplied you with. ✓
7. The sales **figures** have improved month on month since we started discounting. *('Figures' are countable. Here it is followed by the plural form of the verb so must have an -s ending.)*
8. Our revolutionary new product is the result of extensive **research**. *('Research' is an uncountable noun and so is never plural.)*

Mistakes with *which, that, who, whose, where* and *what*

1. What (Use *what* at the beginning of sentences to emphasise the importance of something, e.g. *What I need is more money. What this company should do is invest in IT.*)
2. who (Use *who* to refer to people.)
3. that/which, which (You can usually use either *which* or *that* to refer to the subject of a sentence. After a comma in sentences like this, you can only use *which*, e.g.
   The machine that/which we bought last week has already broken – but the machines we bought before that are OK.
   The machine, ~~that~~/which we bought last week, has already broken – 'which we bought last week' just adds extra information about the machine.)
4. where (*Where* in this case means *in which*.)
5. that (Use *that* when you are reporting what someone said, e.g.
   Health and Safety training will be a priority = *The management has agreed / said / stated that* …)
6. whose (Use *whose* to refer to something relating to or belonging to a person, or sometimes to a thing.)
7. Please return the invoice **that/which** we sent you, as it contains an error. (Look at answer 3 above.)

8 Lausanne Holdings AG have announced **that** they will be opening an office in Paris next year. (Look at answer 5 above.)

9 The conference was held in London, **which** was a very popular choice. (Look at answer 3 above.)

10 I'm afraid I can't help. You'll have to speak to the person **who** is responsible. (Look at answer 2 above.)

11 Prices have fallen to the point **where** production is no longer economic. (Look at answer 4 above.)

12 The new CEO, **who** had only been in the job for six months, was fired suddenly yesterday. (Look at answer 2 above.)

Test practice

The correct line is 3.

2 opportunity (This is referring to one opportunity so the plural form is wrong here.)

4 You agreed <u>that</u> (This is reporting what someone said.)

5 <u>your</u> shop (*Your* shows that something belongs to the person you are talking to, e.g. *Is this your car?* Compare to *Is this car yours?*)

6 we <u>will</u> stock (This is referring to a future fact.)

7 has <u>been</u> placed (This is a passive structure; *has* + *-ing* cannot be correct in this case.)

Reading and Language Knowledge Part 2, Section 6
Test (page 62)

104 has been ~~deciding~~ **decided**
105 ~~has~~ **will** take place
106 date**s**
107 ✓
108 you ~~can~~ **are** subsequently
109 add you ~~at~~ **to** the list
110 if you ~~required~~ **require**

Writing Part 1 Practice (page 64)

Writing practice

1 c, f   **5** l, n
2 b, h   **6** i, k
3 a, e   **7** j, m
4 d, g

Test practice (1 and 2)

Dear Ms Pearson
<u>Thank you for your email</u>[1] regarding re-arranging your interview. I am sorry to hear you have been ill. <u>I would be happy to</u>[2] arrange another time for your interview. <u>Would you be able to</u>[3] come at 3.00 on Monday 15th May? <u>I would be grateful if</u>[4] you could bring a copy of your CV with you to the interview.
Best regards
Michael Kennedy

> *Other possible answers:*
> *1 Thanks for your email*
> *2 I am happy to / We are happy to / We would be pleased to / I would be pleased to / Let's / We can*
> *3 Could you / Can you / Would it be possible for you to*
> *4 It would be helpful if / I wonder if*

Notes about the sample answer:
- This answer includes all three points.
- The main part of the email is 59 words. Don't worry about 'Dear …' and 'Best regards'. They won't be counted.
- Remember that emails can be very informal in English, but when two people do not know each other, formal or neutral language like this is needed.

Writing Part 1 Test (page 65)

Sample answer

Dear Mr Mason
Thank you for your fax. 8.00 is fine for the taxi.
Regarding the equipment for my talk, all I need is a data projector for my laptop.
Would it be possible for you to send me a copy of the conference programme? Thanks for all your help and see you at the conference.
Yours sincerely

[53 words]

Writing Part 2 Practice (page 66)

Writing practice

1 The Managing Director (you should therefore be using formal language).

2 Three points have to be included – why a bigger office is needed, a suitable location and what facilities the new office should have. (Remember: your English is being tested, not your knowledge of business, e.g. it doesn't matter if the office you describe really is a typical business office, but it is important how you use English to describe it.) As it says in the question, you can add other information, but you don't have to. Do not add other information before you have written about the three points in the question.

3 Probably. The question asks you to 'make your recommendations'. Usually, this will be part of your conclusion.

4 As the question says 'Write about 180–200 words.' You should not write more than 200 words because it is not necessary. You will not get a higher grade, so keep to the word limit and if you have any extra time at the end, use it to check your answer for mistakes. Do not worry if your answer is slightly less than 180 words. The examiner will not count the number of words unless the answer looks very short or very long.

Test practice

2 Due to the fact that
3 it was found that
4 This would mean that
5 In addition
6 It is concluded that
7 it is recommended that

Comments on the sample answer:
- The use of grammar and vocabulary is accurate. There are no mistakes in this answer.
- The language here is quite formal and there are some examples of passives used in the conclusion.
- The answer is organised into clear paragraphs with subtitles, e.g. *Why new premises?*
- The ideas are easy to follow. The answer gives reasons for each of the three points and there is linking, e.g. *in addition*.
- All three points are included in the answer. It is a very good answer.

Writing Part 2 Test (page 67)

Sample answer for Task A

Report on travel and entertainment expenses

This report will examine why travel and entertainment expenses have risen so dramatically recently.

Background

A) Travel expenses

Annually this company spends approximately £200,000 on travel. Most of this money covers sales staff within the UK including petrol, accommodation and food expenses. About £60,000 covers overseas travel. Both figures have risen over the last 12 months as we have expanded in the UK and are beginning to launch more products abroad, too.

B) Entertainment expenses

We spent just over £100,000 on entertainment last year including hotel and restaurant costs for domestic clients and overseas visitors.

Although spending on entertainment and travel is growing, this spending is necessary. Our UK customers have always said they prefer personal contact with our sales staff to buying online. If we want to expand abroad, we have to send staff overseas to make new contacts and also to host visits from foreign customers.

We are investigating ways of reducing expenses and have decided it would be possible to replace our current company cars with more economical models. As for flights, we will encourage all managers to use budget airlines where possible and not to fly business class.

[196 words]

Sample answers for Task B

Report on office space in the department

This report aims to investigate problems with office space in the department and how to improve the situation.

Problems of space

It was found that most staff have less than 1.5 metres of desk space each. This is because the number of staff has risen by 25% over the last five years. Also there is more IT equipment being used than in the past, which has further reduced space.

Effects on the department

Due to the fact that staff have less room than before, the department is becoming very untidy as more work is being done in less space as we get busier. This is also having the effect that staff are less happy with their working environment than in the past.

Recommendations

It is not possible to reduce the number of staff to make more space, but we are fortunate that there is a storage room in the department used for keeping old paper records. As our records will all be computerised soon, it will be possible to convert this room into extra office space. It is therefore recommended that we consult an architect as soon as possible.

[196 words]

Speaking Part 1 Practice (page 70)

Test preparation

Useful language

2 a

3 g

4 f

5 c

6 b

7 d

Speaking Part 2 Practice (page 72)

Test practice (sample answers)

Recording scripts

🎧 **22** **Presentation 1**

Candidate 1: I've chosen Topic A: Talk about a meeting you attended. <u>I chose this topic because</u>[1] I had to attend a meeting recently and it was very interesting. The meeting was held in a meeting room in my company and <u>it was about the annual budget for the department</u>[2]. This kind of meeting is very important because the decisions we make at it will affect the way the department works for the next year.

<u>Erm</u>[3], <u>there were eight people at the meeting: me, the head of the department, his deputy and members of the sales team</u>[4] – <u>erm</u>[3], I forgot to say that I work in the sales team – and a secretary taking the minutes.

<u>Well</u>[3], <u>I prepared for the meeting by looking at the minutes for last year's meeting to see if that would give me any useful information</u>[5], but I also looked at my team's spending over the year and tried to predict whether I would need to ask for a bigger budget for them or not.

Examiner: And was the meeting successful?

Candidate 1: Yes, I think it was, because we managed to reach an agreement on the budget much more quickly than last year. I was very pleased.

> [1] This is useful for beginning your presentation.
> [2] Point 1 of question.
> [3] Natural hesitations.
> [4] Point 2 of the question.
> [5] Point 3 of the question.

Did the candidates cover all the points?

🎧 **23** **Presentation 2**

Candidate 2: I want to talk about Topic A. [long pause] Erm, I went to a meeting last week and there were about ten people there. [long pause] Erm, the meeting lasted for about three hours. [long pause] It was very boring. I can't really remember what we talked about. [long pause] Erm, I think it was about money. I didn't have time to prepare for the meeting, because [long pause] I've been very busy at work.

Examiner: And was the meeting successful?

Candidate 2: [long pause] No.

Examiner: Why?

Candidate 2: [long pause] I don't know.

Comments on the sample presentations:

Candidate 1

This is a good answer because:
- the candidate has organised what she says in a way which is easy to follow.
- she says why she chose this topic.
- she talks about all three points in the question.
- she adds some extra information to make it more interesting, but she does not add too much and use up too much time.
- she answers the examiner's follow-up question clearly and gives a reason for the answer.

> Sample answer 1: useful language
>
> I chose this topic because …
> This kind of … is very important because …
> I prepared for the meeting by *-ing* …
> I also …
> I think … , because …

Candidate 2

This is a poor answer because:
- there are too many unnatural hesitations while she searches for words.
- she doesn't talk about all three points.
- she doesn't answer the examiner's question with any detail.
- Remember that the examiner is only interested in how you give your answer. Even if you know very little about the topic, you can still give a good answer to a question.

Practice exercise
2 addition
3 believe
4 else
5 more
6 said
7 well
8 only

Speaking Part 3 Practice (page 74)

Test preparation

Making questions to ask the examiner
job responsibilities: What will my responsibilities be?
salary: Could you tell me what the salary is?
other benefits offered: What other benefits will the company give me?

Preparing for the discussion
1 a, f
2 c, h
3 d, g
4 b, e

BULATS Answer Sheet

Family name: ....
First name(s): ....
Centre number: ☐☐☐☐☐

Candidate number:

| 0 1 2 3 4 5 6 7 8 9 |
| 0 1 2 3 4 5 6 7 8 9 |
| 0 1 2 3 4 5 6 7 8 9 |
| 0 1 2 3 4 5 6 7 8 9 |
| 0 1 2 3 4 5 6 7 8 9 |
| 0 1 2 3 4 5 6 7 8 9 |

Candidate organisation: ....

Test language: English ▭ French ▭ German ▭ Spanish ▭

Version number:
▶ 0 1 2 3 4 5 6 7 8 9
▶ 0 1 2 3 4 5 6 7 8 9

Test date (shade ONE box for the day, ONE box for the month and ONE box for the year)

Day: 01 02 03 04 05 06 07 08 09 10 11 12 13 14 15 16 17 18 19 20 21 22 23 24 25 26 27 28 29 30 31

Month: 01 02 03 04 05 06 07 08 09 10 11 12   Last digit of the Year: 0 1 2 3 4 5 6 7 8 9

Please complete details above, then read instructions on other side of this sheet before you begin.

Listening

Part 1

1	A B C
2	A B C
3	A B C
4	A B C
5	A B C
6	A B C
7	A B C
8	A B C
9	A B C
10	A B C

Part 2

		Do not write here
11		1 11 0
12		1 12 0
13		1 13 0
14		1 14 0
15		1 15 0
16		1 16 0
17		1 17 0
18		1 18 0
19		1 19 0
20		1 20 0
21		1 21 0
22		1 22 0

Part 3

23	A B C D E F G H I
24	A B C D E F G H I
25	A B C D E F G H I
26	A B C D E F G H I
27	A B C D E F G H I
28	A B C D E F G H I
29	A B C D E F G H I
30	A B C D E F G H I
31	A B C D E F G H I
32	A B C D E F G H I

Part 4

33	A B C	39	A B C	45	A B C
34	A B C	40	A B C	46	A B C
35	A B C	41	A B C	47	A B C
36	A B C	42	A B C	48	A B C
37	A B C	43	A B C	49	A B C
38	A B C	44	A B C	50	A B C

Answer sheet continues.
Please turn over ➡

Reading and Language Knowledge – Part One

Part 1.1
51	A B C
52	A B C
53	A B C
54	A B C
55	A B C
56	A B C
57	A B C

Part 1.2
58	A B C D
59	A B C D
60	A B C D
61	A B C D
62	A B C D
63	A B C D

Part 1.3
64	A B C
65	A B C
66	A B C
67	A B C
68	A B C
69	A B C

Part 1.4

	Do not write here
70	1 70 0
71	1 71 0
72	1 72 0
73	1 73 0
74	1 74 0

Reading and Language Knowledge – Part Two

Part 2.1
75	A B C D
76	A B C D
77	A B C D
78	A B C D
79	A B C D
80	A B C D
81	A B C D

Part 2.2
82	A B C D
83	A B C D
84	A B C D
85	A B C D
86	A B C D

Part 2.3
	Do not write here
87	1 87 0
88	1 88 0
89	1 89 0
90	1 90 0
91	1 91 0

Part 2.4
92	A B C D
93	A B C D
94	A B C D
95	A B C D
96	A B C D
97	A B C D

Part 2.5
98	A B C D
99	A B C D
100	A B C D
101	A B C D
102	A B C D
103	A B C D

Part 2.6
	Do not write here
104	1 104 0
105	1 105 0
106	1 106 0
107	1 107 0
108	1 108 0
109	1 109 0
110	1 110 0

Instructions:

Use a PENCIL (B or HB). Rub out any answer you wish to change with an eraser.

For **Multiple-choice:** Mark ONE letter for each question. For example, if you think **C** is the right answer to the question, mark your answer sheet like this:

0 | A B C D

For **written answers:** Write your answers in the spaces next to the numbers like this:

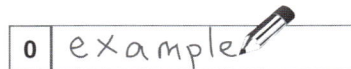

0 | example

Acknowledgements

David Clark would like to thank his editors, Sue Ashcroft and Shona Rodger, for all their help and support throughout this project.

The authors and publishers would like to thank the teachers who commented on the material:

China: Ronald Wedin; France: Sylvie Bayle, Patricia Chaix, Eunice Nyhan; Germany: Philip Moore, Jürgen Quetz, Joanna Westcombe; Hong Kong: Michihiro Hirai, Mark Knight; Italy: Peter Anderson, Adrian James; Japan: Brent Conkle; Spain: Caroline Cooke; UK: Elaine Allen, Paul Bress, Bruce Howell, Ros Smith.

The authors and publishers are grateful to the authors, publishers and others who have given permission for the use of copyright material identified in the text. It has not been possible to identify the sources of all the material used and in such cases the publishers would welcome information from copyright owners. Apologies are expressed for any omissions.

Text on p 36 from Crimson Business at www.startups.co.uk © Crimson Business; text on p 50 from *Management Today* August 2004, courtesy of Management Today (MT Magazine), www.mtmagazine.co.uk; text on p 57 from *Business: The Ultimate Resource*, by Michael Griggs and Maggie Kennedy, used by permission of Bloomsbury Publishing plc.

Produced by Kamae Design, Oxford

Cover design by:
OptaDesign

Illustrations by:
John Storey and Kamae Design